FIND IT, FILE IT, FLOG IT

PHARMA'S CRIPPLING ADDICTION AND HOW TO CURE IT

D1508987

Hedley G Rees

ISBN-13: 9781514261217
ISBN-10: 1514261219
Library of Congress Control Number: 2015919394
CreateSpace Independent Publishing Platform
North Charleston, South Carolina

FIND IT, FILE IT, FLOG IT

TABLE OF CONTENTS

To

Carol, my wife and best friend, who raised me up to more that I can be.
Our daughters, Carley and Katie, who luckily inherited Carol's looks, not mine.
Martyn, my son, who keeps me appraised on all matters sport.
Gereint and Josh, respective husband and boyfriend to our daughters.
Ellie and Emilia, the cutest, cuddliest granddaughters in the world.
Morfydd and Jack, my late parents; hopefully, they are smiling down on us.

PREFACE

I almost didn't write this book. My maiden attempt at a book, despite great reviews, was a disappointment in terms of sales. I had been certain the world was hungry to hear the messages within, not just to inform and educate on my speciality subject—strategic management of the supply chain—but also to help catalyze change for the better in the pharmaceutical industry. As I think back, the important messages were disguised within a relatively high-priced textbook in an industry where the topic of professional management of end-to-end supply chains was as popular as the Conservative Club in Moscow.

Undeterred, I continued to preach the messages at conferences, in professional journals, and through webcasts and podcasts. The presentation I gave at conferences in the United States and European Union was purposefully provocative. I resorted to giving the drug development and commercialization process a funny name, Find It, File It, Flog It, and semiridiculing the notion of scientists discovering blockbuster drugs in the dead of night, surrounded by test tubes, Bunsen burners and other apparatus involved in deep chemistry.

The audiences were always polite. No one challenged me on what I said, although there must have been a lot of skepticism underneath. The only manifestation of that was when I presented at a conference in Tuscany, where a senior Food and Drug Administration official had a coughing fit halfway through my presentation and had to leave. She did not return until I had finished.

I toyed with the idea of writing something more direct and explicit than my first attempt, accessible to the "informed patient" as well as those in the industry. Something was stopping me, though. It was one thing shouting at the dark and accepting that no one was interested, but totally different about an industry seemingly so privileged and well established.

Then I read *The War of Art* by Steven Pressfield. His view was that creativity is blood, sweat, and tears and a fight against the fear of creating something at which others will pick. It requires a steely determination to keep resisting the knot in your stomach telling you to stop and pursue more tranquil endeavors—to turn up at your desk every morning to write the next installment.

I didn't stop, and this book is the result. I hope you enjoy it. I certainly enjoyed writing it—in the end.

Acknowledgements

There are so many to thank that the list could make up another book. First on the list is Donna Ladkin PhD, professor of leadership and ethics at Cranfield School of Management. Professor Ladkin supervised my MBA project at Cranfield and was effusive in her praise of the content. Her validation of my work gave me so much confidence in the potential for my skills as an author. I thanked Cranfield University School of Management in my last book. I am still eternally grateful for that life-changing experience.

Next to thank is Robert Mansfield, former CEO of Vanguard Medica and Neuropharm. He put an exceptional team of people together at Vanguard, which I was asked to join, and subsequently employed me as consultant to Neuropharm in 2007. It was there where I first met Marla Phillips, PhD, who came over from the United States to Swindon in the UK, to carry out a Good Manufacturing Practice audit on one of Neuropharm's manufacturing contractors. Shortly afterward, she moved to take a position as director of Xavier Health at Xavier University, where she asked me to help her with one of her conferences—the FDA/Xavier University cosponsored Global Outsourcing Conference, first as a speaker and then as cochair from 2011 to 2014. This conference has grown, and its name has changed to PharmaLink.

Through this conference, Marla introduced me to many people, notably Professor Jim O'Reilly and Bob Coleman. Professor O'Reilly is a legend in the world of FDA law, and he gave my previous book tremendous reviews. Mr. Coleman is a legend also, in the world of implementing

FDA law, as a former inspector and as a national drug expert. He was kind enough to write the back cover review for my previous book. Kathleen Culver, preapproval inspection manager at the FDA's Cincinnati District and the other cochair of the conference, consistently captured the audience's attention with her tales of "horror" from the real world of pharmaceutical inspections. Although her stories were always entertaining, they had a serious message behind them.

Steve Eastham, supervisor of the Consumer Safety Office at the FDA's Cincinnati District, was unwavering in his support for the establishment and growth of the conference way above the call of duty. Steve Niedelman, deputy associate commissioner for regulatory affairs at the FDA for more than thirty-four years and now lead quality systems and compliance consultant at King & Spalding, was a tower of strength with whom I shared the common bond of grandfatherhood.

The rest of the strategic committee, you know who you are and that I enjoyed working with you, are too numerous to mention by name, and I hope you forgive me for referring to you in the aggregate.

I also thank Deb Autor during her time as director of office of compliance at the FDA Center for Drug Evaluation and Research. Ms. Autor was a breath of fresh air when heading up the office of compliance when it was made a "super office" and was always willing to help me with queries or point me in the right direction. Steve Lynn, as FDAs director of product manufacturing and quality, was always happy to chat about matters patient safety and quality. We shared the podium a number of times, and he kindly included some of my work in his presentations.

On the other side of the pond, I should acknowledge Mark Birse, Group Manager Inspectorate at the Medicines and Healthcare Products Regulatory Agency (MHRA) for sharing his expert opinion at the Pharmalink 2014 conference, responding to my queries or requests for help and most importantly, being a key mover in the new era of global regulatory collaboration which has clearly emerged; also Ian Rees, Unit Manager Inspectorate Strategy and Innovation at MHRA, for advice when requested; also other MHRA speakers at Pharmalink, namely Richard Andrews, Unit Manager - Inspectorate Operations, Rachel Carmichael, former MHRA Inspector, now Executive Director at NSF Health Sciences

Pharma Biotech Consulting and David Churchward, Expert GMDP Inspector at MHRA.

Thanks go also to those who published my work, Paul Tunnah at Pharmaphorum; Gareth McDonald at In-PharmaTechnologist; Agnes Shanley while at Putman Media, Contract Pharma magazine and UBM Advanstat Communications; Robyn Barnes at MasterControl and Martin Van Trieste, SVP Quality Amgen, who organized reprinting of one of my PharmaPhorum articles in the Rx-360 newsletter.

Next thanks go to Nick Rodgers, Chairman of Oxford BioMedica. As fortune would have it, we shared a table at the launch of the UKs advanced manufacturing supply chain initiative (AMSCI), Round 3 in London, after which he facilitated my appointment as consultant on the bid; also thanks to Mark Bustard, Head of Medical Biotechnology at UKs Knowledge Transfer Network, for engaging me to attend the AMSCI launch meeting, with a view to finding life science companies willing to bid, after none had been successful in the previous two rounds. James Christie, Director of Manufacturing at Oxford BioMedica, was great to work with and Tim Watts, Finance Director, was a tower of strength in navigating the complexities of funding do's and don't's.

I am grateful to David Norrington of Onion Custard Publishing, who's 'Author's Discovery Day' provided valuable insights into the world of self publishing and who gave me the confidence to run with the title Find It, File It, Flog It. I owe a great debt of thanks to Piper Terrett, free-lance journalist and founder of The Frugal Life Blog, who helped shape and develop the important messages in the book, remove many a grammatical faux pas, and generally kept me on track during the foundation stage of the manuscript.

Finally, a huge thank you goes to the Expert Witnesses, who had no idea how this was going to turn out when I first approached them to contribute, and yet were still willing to lay their views on the line.

CHAPTER 1

ABOUT THIS BOOK

Why should you read this book?

You should not read this book if you are not an investor, executive, or lawyer in the industry. If you have never been a professional working in drug research, development, commercial supply, finance, marketing, or all of the other disciplines operating in the sector, this book should not find its way onto your shelves. If you are not a health-care professional, nurse, doctor, surgeon, medical auxiliary, for example, this book is not for you. Most important, if you are not or have never been a patient, these pages should remain closed to you.

For those still with us, there is much in this book for you. Investors are first on the list because they are likely to benefit most in terms of return on investment and risk reduction, while driving much-needed improvements. Executives will sleep more soundly at night as they face the world with a newfound mission in life. Lawyers will get tons more satisfaction from their fee-earning hours while earning a sizable crust.

Professionals in the industry will realize that they have been marching to the wrong beat and learn what's needed to readjust their steps. They will become reenergized with prospects and opportunities they do not know exist. Health-care professionals will learn how to bring companies developing pharmaceutical therapies into alignment with their needs, as they finally reconnect with the medicines they prescribe.

For patients, the ultimate benefactors of this book, there is so much to discover. The complexities of the pharmaceutical maze will be unearthed, the myths about the cost of drug development and time to market will be debunked, and a new set of insights will put patients, finally, in control of their own destinies as receivers of medicine.

In summary, you are all in for a massive eye-opener—a peek into the inner workings of an industry in crisis, struggling to come to terms with errors of the past and predicaments of the present. You will learn about the industry's gambling addiction of the early 1980s and discover the debilitating state of this gambler in denial.

It is not all doom and gloom, of course, but the prognosis is dire and the road to recovery is hard—very hard. Fundamental change is required if Pharma's future is to turn the corner.

Is this just another swipe at Big Pharma?

This is absolutely not another swipe at Big Pharma. It is a laser-guided missile into the nerve center of an industry shrouded in mystery. It aims to blast away the ironclad armor and the smoke and mirrors that have bedeviled the industry for more than several decades. Throughout, it is based on evidence. Although some may be circumstantial, there are more than enough facts and testimony to provide a fair hearing for all. It goes far further than raising issues; it sets out a plan that could return Big Pharma to its former glory.

At this point, we should introduce the term "Big Pharma," as it is used widely in the industry. For those not familiar with the term, it means the global research and development (R&D)-based companies that develop and supply medicine, medical devices, diagnostic tests, and other health-care products on the market. The number-one spot changes with merger and acquisition activity, but as of September 2015, it is held by Johnson & Johnson. Pfizer, Novartis, Merck and GSK have also held the top spot.

Big Pharma has always been the alpha male of the pharmaceutical industry. No plan is going to succeed if it does not recognize and address the behaviors of these beasts within the overall context of the 'troop' that makes up the various business models and actors in the pharmaceutical industry of today. This is why the central focus of this book will be on the role of Big Pharma in dictating the industry dynamic. This is not based on allocating blame to Big Pharma or any other player in the world of pharmaceuticals. The plan is based on a systems view of the world, whereby blame and searching for culprits are counterproductive to the ultimate objective. The great Doctor Deming taught us that systems, not people, let us down in the vast majority of cases. Without a clear view of the dependencies and interrelationships in any system, we can easily make matters worse while trying to do the right thing. We will therefore focus on how key stakeholders unwittingly contribute to the issues and how they can contribute to the solution.

The journey through the book

The book begins by looking back in time, to when all is rosy in the Big Pharma garden and life is sweet. The telltale signs of complacency and blind optimism were there even in those days, but nothing could beat the life it had found for itself.

Looking to improve an already comfortable lifestyle, Big Pharma companies cast off their assets to focus on core activities and in the process planted the seeds of poison that took root. An in-depth review of the symptoms reveals a shocking truth. Big Pharma is sick, very sick—and the prognosis is not good. Addiction is never easy to conquer.

We then take a long, hard look at where things are today—a reality check. We strip away any hype, wishful thinking, and blind optimism. This topic is too important to pull punches. Then we take a visit back to basics and the unspoken assumptions that have driven the industry to where it is today. Finally, we visit a new set of assumptions and ideas that could transform the industry, exploring novel ways for all of the key stakeholders to play their parts in meaningful change for the better.

Will the book be difficult to read?

I hope not. With precious little knowledge of biology, I barely know one end of a test tube from the other. Experts who taught me over the years had to massively simplify concepts so I could understand them. I will use that simplification process for those who need it.

There will also be three easy to read sections to break up any monotony, starting with:

A HELPFUL METAPHOR

> *"The greatest thing by far is to be a master of metaphor."*
> —*Aristotle*

I'm not picking fights with Aristotle when it comes to logic, so I'm taking his word for it. Metaphors interspersed throughout the book may help readers identify with the issues and concerns.

AN EXPERT WITNESS STATEMENT

These are accounts from people who have been there, done that, and become experts in their respective fields. The unifying factor is that all of them are desperate to see change in the industry—not just tweaks and work-arounds, but rather root-and-branch transformations.

I have handpicked these people, whom I have encountered at some stage in my career. Their views have resonated with mine, albeit they are far more expert in their respective fields. Included in the list are members of my LinkedIn group, Friends of Modernization in the Drug Industry. I started this discussion group in 2011 as a way of sharing thoughts and ideas on the regulatory approaches to modernization that had been on the agenda for quite some time. Many in the group are experts in quality by design and process analytical technology. You can find short biographies in the appendix; sound bites from their contributions follow below, in alphabetical order.

"I believe there needs to be a radical realignment of the framework, or rather straightjacket, which currently constrains the drug development process"

Dr Gary Acton
Captain, Pirates of Oncology, creative and communicative cancer clinician.

Former Chief Medical Officer, Antisoma Research Ltd.

"I challenge industry to get close to their customers, stakeholders, try to walk in their shoes, understand the complexities of the part of the system they work in. "

Mrs Bethan Bishop
Project Director, Creative Digital Health Solutions, Heart of England NHS Foundation Trust.
Steering Committee Member - Advanced Manufacturing Supply Chain Initiative, Oxford BioMedica.
Former Head of Innovation & Industry Engagement, Heart of England NHS Foundation Trust.

"Unfortunately for the major Pharmaceutical companies that used to be the 'channel captains', who controlled the industry and all of its major supply chains through a judicious control internally of critical assets, there has been considerable evidence of very poor practice in outsourcing in recent years"

Professor Andrew Cox
Chairman of Advisory Board & Vice President, International Institute for Advanced Purchasing & Supply.
Former Professor of Business Strategy & Procurement, University of Birmingham Business School.

"With only 1 in 4 launched drugs ever repaying its R&D cost, the logic and justification for this huge market research spend would seem to be driven more by historic cultural precedent rather than directing good business decision making. "

Dr Graham Cox
Principal Consultant, KASOCIO Limited.
Former Global Strategic Planning VP, AstraZeneca.

"Unfortunately, the pharmaceutical industry, almost like a religion, cherished "tradition" over change or modern ideas. When formulation and production of tablets and capsules moved from the back rooms of the corner pharmacy to industrial plants, it brought baggage, er, uh, I mean traditions. "

5

Emil Ciurczak
Independent Pharmaceuticals Professional, Doramaxx Consulting.
Contributing Editor for Pharmaceutical Manufacturing.

"The lesson advanced therapy medicinal product (ATMP) developers need to learn is 'know your customer', and develop a product that meets all their needs in addition to clinical efficacy".

Dr Drew Hope
CRF GMP Unit Head of ATMP Quality at Guy's and St. Thomas' NHS Foundation Trust.
Former Regulation Manager, UK Human Tissue Authority.

"The (lack of) resilience of global pharmaceutical supply chain networks has been laid bare in recent years by the global drug shortage crisis"

Mrs Catherine Geyman
Director, Intersys Ltd.
Former Risk Management Consultant, AstraZeneca.

"I worked in the generic drug industry for OTC products and can tell you that there are differences between branded drugs and generics."

Richard Meyer
Chief Strategy Officer, Online Strategic Solutions.
Former Senior Marketing Manager, Medtronic-Diabetes.

"Now imagine you set objectives at the business level and you express these vital objectives as a challenge to every manager in the business – not as individuals – but as a whole!"

Professor Nick Rich
Professor of Socio-Technical Systems Design (Operations Management), School of Management, Swansea University.
Honorary Professor, Warwick Medical School.
Co-founder of the Lean Enterprise Research Centre at Cardiff Business School.

Pharma might spend lots of money on R&D but the evidence suggests that it is simply not effective."

Professor Daniel Steenstra
Royal Academy of Engineering Visiting Professor in Medical Innovation, Cranfield University.
Steering Committee Member - Advanced Manufacturing Supply Chain Initiative, Oxford BioMedica.

"I need to say that the Industry must grow up. It needs to move away from the child-parent relationship it has allowed to develop with the regulators. Waiting to be told what to do, by regulators and the ensuing consultants, isn't a good sign of organisational capability or a mature culture."

Peter Savin
Editor at GMP Review, Euromed Communications.
Former VP, Global Quality Assurance, GlaxoSmithKline.

"Too many of our drugs are basically expensive me-too drugs that offer minimal, if any, advantages over earlier compounds. Physicians know this and patients eventually figure it out and can't understand why their doctor is making them pay so much for so little"

Jack Shapiro
Owner, Shapiro Healthcare Marketing Research.
Former Director, Market Research, Ayerst Laboratories.

*"Big Pharma changed strategy and started to hire **sales**-people for their field-forces. Someone had come up with the idea that "selling" delivers more than helping physicians to make the best possible therapeutic choice, consult, advise, and share the huge Pharma disease know-how with prescribers."*

Hanno Wolfram
Owner, Innov8 GmbH.
Co-Founder, Pharmainstitut.
Former Principal EMEA, Learning Solutions & Change Management, IMS.

"The industry still largely relies on a semi-random trial-and-error process for developing new therapeutic products. This is particularly the case in the development of biopharmaceuticals (protein-based drugs), where most current handicaps derive from the traditional 'linear' hierarchical methodology, in which different stages of drug development operate under almost complete isolation from one another, making it very difficult (and expensive) to solve problems once they are detected."

Jesús Zurdo
Senior Director, Strategic Innovation, Pharma & Biotech, Lonza.
Former Head of Innovation, Biopharma Development, Lonza.

ENDS

The final perspective interspersed through the book will be mine:

VIEWS, OBSERVATIONS, AND PERSONAL EXPERIENCES OF THE AUTHOR

These will describe my personal observations while working in the bowels of this industry for a long time. These should be of value to readers because I've spent time in what I call my three phases of enlightenment: working for the large Pharmaceutical companies (Big Pharma), small companies developing drugs (biotech/virtual) and as a consultant working along the end-to-end supply chain from early-stage discovery to supply across global markets.

Very briefly, and not to lose you to an afternoon nap, here they are described:

Life in Big Pharma (large R&D-based pharmaceutical companies)

It was fortunate for me that in late 1979, I joined a company that Bayer AG (Miles Laboratories) recently acquired and benefited enormously from learning in a leading multinational corporation with top-notch training and work systems. I also learned much about the industry modus operandi and the omnipotence of R&D, the dreadful inertia against change and the straitjacket of regulations. It was a move into the world of drug development in 1996.

Life in Drug Development
I spent nearly ten years working at the sharp end of drug development, helping get products over the valley of death, working with some of the best in the field who had left Big Pharma, either through choice or forcibly. My eyes truly opened here.

Then it was a move into life as a supply-chain consultant in 2005.

Life as an Independent Consultant
In November 2004, after having headed OSI Pharmaceuticals' supply chain for the successful launch of Tarceva (a drug to treat non-small-cell lung cancer) in the United States, I joined the many contractors in the industry who had been displaced, as OSI closed part of its operation in the United Kingdom. Armed with a bright new website, tons of enthusiasm for supply-chain management (my specialty subject) and a relatively successful track record, I set about building a business in a land where, as I was to find out, supply chains and their effectiveness were the last things on anyone's mind.

Through 2005, I managed to talk with a few CEOs of companies at Milton Park in Oxfordshire UK which was a hotbed of biotech activity close to where I had been working.

One visit sticks out boldly in my mind. It was the point where I realized that I may have made a big mistake moving into the supply-chain management consultancy field targeting small drug developers. Their hearts weren't in their supply chains.

VIEWS, OBSERVATIONS, AND PERSONAL EXPERIENCES OF THE AUTHOR
This particular CEO I visited said he would see me for a couple of hours. If he liked what he heard, then some work could come out of it. As we progressed through the meeting, it became clear that the CEO was explaining to me why what I offered was of no interest because he was aiming to make an exit once proof of concept was achieved. The chance to exit would be based almost entirely on the clinical efficacy data, and the supply chain would be someone else's problem.

9

He also predicted that no other CEO in a similar position would take notice. He even drew me a graph to drive the knife further firmly between the ribs.

ENDS

I'm not looking for sympathy for the experience. The message I aim to convey is the presence and depth of a mind-set ingrained into the industry psyche. The CEO was not wrong in his prediction of a lack of his peers' interest in building and properly managing supply chains for the future.

Here, we have it. We start with a look back to the early days of the Pharmaceutical industry.

PART I PHARMA PAST

CHAPTER 2

It wasn't always like this

It has recently struck me that the pharmaceutical industry for many people has always been the same as it is today. A trade journal reporter declaring "Pharma has traditionally been business-to-business" confirmed this realization. This is certainly not the case, and those of more mature years, such as myself, remember a different time. The reporter's comment made me wonder how this perception occurred and how widespread it was. If the misconception is common, then I should explain.

When today's drug companies were in their infancies, probably in the 1950s, things were very different. GlaxoSmithKline (then Glaxo) started by making powdered milk for babies. Beecham's (now GlaxoSmithKline) was famous for its flu powders, Johnson & Johnson was famous for baby hair shampoo, and Novartis wasn't even a twinkle in its grandfather's eye. Blockbusters hadn't been invented, and Big Pharma companies generally had clear views of the customer constituencies they were serving.

All had an underpinning focus on the need to satisfy patients first. The words of George W. Merck, the founder of Merck & Co, provides evidence:

"We try never to forget that medicine is for the people. It is not for the profits. The profits follow, and if we have remembered that, they have never failed to appear. The better we have remembered it, the larger they have been!"

Are these words now lost in the mists of time? We hope to find out as we progress.

VIEWS, OBSERVATIONS, AND PERSONAL EXPERIENCES OF THE AUTHOR

During my early days at Bayer manufacturing in Wales, the manufacturing and supply process was pretty much integrated, from the point where raw materials arrived at the back door and the finished product was made and sent directly to customers—hospitals, Pharmacies, and sometimes patients—in the home market and to other Bayer entities around the globe. Those Bayer entities had local presence and distribution capabilities in their own home markets. Links with customers were direct, and the staff at Bayer, the company holding the license to sell the products, could handle customer complaints.

The staff making Alka Seltzer for Europe had a standing joke. A polystyrene packing piece was at the top of each glass bottle as a cushion to prevent the tablets from moving and breaking. It was a frequent occurrence for customers to send the piece back to the plant with a complaint that it wouldn't dissolve. The reply was always polite and understanding, but It was hard to resist a wry smile.

ENDS

That was life before the blockbuster era. Let's go back to the days of Big Pharma as a little boy in short trousers.

Rich pickings begin

Pickings began to get rich starting in the mid-1970s, mostly from the battle of the stomach ulcer drugs Tagamet (Smith Kline & French) and Zantac (Glaxo). Even though Tagamet was the first to market (1976), Zantac overtook Tagamet soon after its launch in 1981 with what was reported to be a superior marketing effort. This seems to have been the birth of the blockbuster era.

By the early 1980s, industry players learned that a patented compound—new molecular entity—with an important license to sell could use nimble marketing to make huge profits under the shelter of patent protection. The industry focused increasingly on patenting as many compounds as seemed reasonable, selected the most promising for development, and then marketed the bones out of them once approved.

Below is a tongue-in-cheek description of the approach. Figure 1 shows a gifted scientist who has found a compound from the patent library that is showing some promise in the test tube. He's having an 'eureka' moment.

Figure 1. The reigning paradigm of drug development (courtesy Expert Witness Dr Graham Cox for the cartoons)

We see that our eager scientist phones his boss, who is under pressure from above to move compounds into development, and he is more than happy to hear the news that the finding has potential. The race is now on to get the magic powder into trials by making larger quantities to test on animals. Figure 2 shows the scientist's baby hastily passed along the development conveyor belt as the patent clock ticks.

Figure 2. The patent clock is ticking

The scientist moves on to find further medical breakthroughs—or not, as the case may be. Other scientists take over the baton and head toward the finish line. The next step is proving that this compound is safe for clinical trials to begin and has some scientific rationale as to why it is going to work.

In the name of conserving remaining patent life, the industry puts things on fast-forward. The patent fairy (or is it a wicked witch?) is omnipresent, and every pause for thought must be met with a poke of her broom handle or a whack with the bristles.

To recap in the real world, this "lifestyle" approach involved finding a promising patented compound (Find It), placing it into a development pipeline intended for regulatory approval to market (File It), and then marketing the approved product with the utmost verve and vigor (Flog It). In mathematical terms, we have:

$$F1 + F2 + F3 = \$\$\$.$$

Where:

F1 = Drug discovery (Find it)
F2 = Regulatory review and approval (File it)
F3 = Marketing (Flog it)

$$$ = Megabucks

This is the equation that has driven the industry ever since—with devastating outcomes. From here on, we will refer to this approach of drug development and commercialization as Triple F, as we continue our exploration of the pharmaceutical industry.

The race to the clinic begins

We now dig more deeply into the "File It" stage, where Pharma companies must prove their compounds are fit to be marketed. We pick up where "Find It" is completed, where a fresh team of scientists takes over from our discovery friends above. They will be conscious of the wicked witch's presence from years of conditioning. A day lost in development is a day's patent life and, more important, lots of money in lost sales if it's a blockbuster. Minds are concentrated appropriately. It's time to get cracking with preclinical testing.

A Helpful Metaphor

Dafydd Morgan got up from the kitchen table to answer the knock at the farmhouse door. Standing on the opposite side of the door was a strangely dressed man with a cloak around his shoulders. He explained that he was a prince consort from a far-off land. With a concerned look on his face, he explained that his people were vegetarian but some were getting sick from a diet lacking in protein. The wise men had researched the issue and concluded that a diet including meat was the only treatment and that Welsh pork sausages were the best. He asked if the Morgan farm would be interested in supplying them with prime sausages.

Dafydd invited the man in to meet his father, Morgan Morgan, and his mother, Morfydd. The prince consort explained what was needed.

Meat was new to them, so they had to be sure it did not upset their delicate tummies. This meant feeding raw pork to their cows, which also were used to vegetarian diets. The cows may not like the pork, but it would be a good sign if they could stomach it.

Then they would feed the sausages in skins to the young, healthy soldiers in the army. They would be the ones least likely to suffer any permanent damage from the experience.

Afterward, a small number of the ailing people would sample some sausages. If it seemed they were beginning to return to health, they would sample more. In the end, if their condition was improving, no tummies were upset, and the sausages were made to princely standards defined by royalty, then sausages could go on sale to those in need.

In return, the prince consort said, the queen, who was a principled lady, would ensure that only sausages from the Morgan farm could be sold to her subjects for the following ten years.

So it began. The Morgan family hired extended family, friends, most of the village, and those farther afield to find the pigs, develop the sausages, send all of the information to the prince consort's office, and do the thousand and one other things necessary to get these sausages approved and on the market. Figure 3 shows how it began:

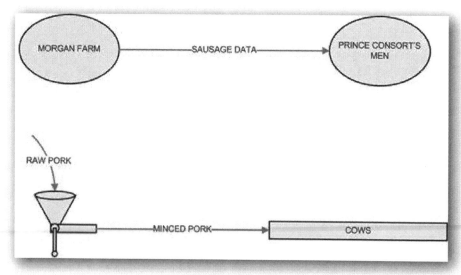

Figure 3. Testing the sausage meat in cows

The raw pork was minced and sent to the far off land to be fed to the cows. The data on how the pork was made and it's effect on the cows were carefully collected and sent to the prince consort's men.

A thumbs up from the prince consorts men leads onto the next stage shown in figure 4

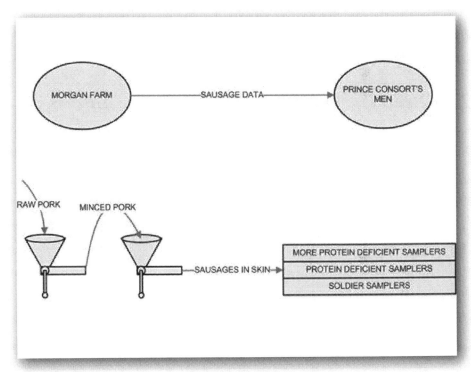

Figure 4. Testing sausages in skins on humans

The minced pork was filled into skins to be fed to samplers in the far off land. A few of the soldiers suffered minor stomach upsets, but nothing too concerning. The subsequent sampling in the protein deficient folk went well, as quite a number of them reported feeling better after a few weeks of downing the sausages.

A review of the data by the price consort's men brought wonderful news—the sausages were succulent and approved for sale! Figure 5 shows how it all meshed together:

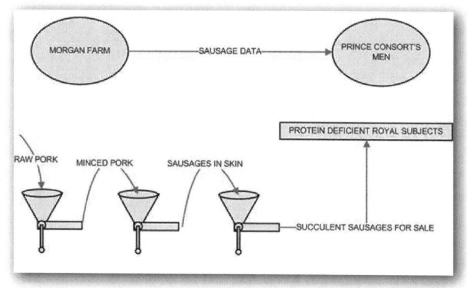

Figure 5. Selling succulent sausages to royal subjects

The project was a great success, and because the kingdom was very rich, the Morgans were paid handsomely for their work and did not have to worry about other families filling the sausage orders for a long time to come. They had more money coming in than they could ever have imagined, and they shared it with all involved.

ENDS

The basics of drug development

Using the metaphor, we are able to shine a light on the basics of drug development. Drugs (new molecular entities) selected as candidates for market have to be proved safe to test in humans. This is what is known as preclinical testing. It involves proving that the drug is tolerated sufficiently well in animals to give a high level of assurance that it can be tested in healthy human volunteers without causing undue or irreversible harm. There is also an attempt to gather evidence that the drug could be effective in the particular disease state under investigation, but animals are much different from humans, so this is always sketchy at best and useless at worst. There is normally a requirement, though, for scientific rationale as to why the drug should work in theory.

The sausage machine is a vital component of the whole system because it is physically what will be doing the magic work during clinical trials and when the drug hits the market. The drug to be fed to animals is less pure than subsequent manufacture of the active ingredient for humans. This is known in the jargon as a "dirty batch." The logic is clear: as development proceeds, each subsequent batch becomes increasingly pure. The dirty batch is the "worst case," and if the regulators are happy for a company to use it for initial testing, the process will be easier.

If the preclinical phase gets approval, the company receives a licence to run clinical trials in humans. This is known as a clinical trial application in the European Union and an investigational new drug in the United States.

Phase I is testing in healthy volunteers. All the data necessary are collected and the results assessed. Every clinical study must have an end point that determines whether the study achieves what it has set out to prove. If it meets its end point, then it can progress to the next stage.

Phase II is sometimes split into an A and a B run in patients with the condition. Information is collected and, again, the company judges, through statistical analysis of the results, whether the study has met its end point. If it has, Phase III testing begins with a mission to gain approval from the regulators to market. If the regulators give approval, then it is hats in the air, yachts on order, and succulent sausages all around!

This was how Tagamet, Zantac, and other blockbusters emerged on the market.

This created another mathematical formula for Big Pharma companies to adopt:

$$S1 + S2 + S3 = \$\$\$$$

21

Where:

S1 = Safe sausage (preclinical testing)
S2 = Sample sausage (clinical trials)
S3 = Succulent sausage (marketing approval)

$$$ = Megabucks

As the years rolled on, increasing numbers of Big Pharma companies had success applying this formula. They became known as R&D-based Pharma companies or Big Pharma for short. This is the name we will use from here on.

The formula is still the basis for the drug development paradigm of today.

CHAPTER 3

BIG PHARMA JETTISONS ITS ASSETS

Success smells so sweet

Success created a thirst for bigger and better returns. Financial whiz kids, consultants, and heaven knows whoever else waded in to provide much-needed advice. By the time Big Pharma was in full swing toward the later 1980s, many sectors had identified the potential benefits associated with outsourcing activities that previously had been carried out in-house. The rationale was simple. If specialist companies can offer services more efficiently and cost effectively than the company can provide for itself, why not let these experts do it, so the focus and profit potential stays firmly on your company's strengths? If it's good enough for them, they thought, then it's good enough for us. This next installment of our metaphor considered what happened in the analogous world of sausages.

A Helpful Metaphor

After the Morgans' success, Evan Evans-Bevan, the village bank manager, paid the family a visit. Mr. Evans-Bevan took pride in his financial prowess that he learned from a course in the big city. He had some interesting advice for the family.

"Now that you've got all this money coming in, he said, you must capitalize on it. That's what all the financial kids in the city say: money has to work for you. Now, I've been through your accounts, and you have an awful lot of money tied up in these sausage machines. I also noticed that if you don't have any work going through the machines, they are lying idle. And why are you filling the sausage machine with all these products for which the prince pays us a pittance after the ten years are up?

"I'm telling you, Morgan boyo, this is all a big mistake. You could be using that money to find lots of different types of sausages and keep the queen and her subjects sweet. They can go on buying, and the money will keep rolling in. It's a faultless plan, man."

Morgan, Dafydd and Morfydd looked at Evan Evans-Bevan as if he were some kind of god. He was a powerful man in the village. They also sensed a strange foreboding in their stomachs as they contemplated the task ahead. Nearly everyone in the village worked for them and a significant number from the surrounding counties within the principality, but they agreed to follow the plan in the name of progress, and the carnage began.

ENDS

It started innocuously enough

As the industry began to dismantle its metaphorical sausage machines, along with those working them, and hand them over to others, the picture changed starkly. It started innocuously enough. The first to go were order taking and cash collection for finished products, warehousing and transportation to hospitals and community Pharmacies. The Pharmaceutical wholesalers and third-party logistics providers (3PLs) of the time began to snap up the assets on offer.

Next to go were the manufacturing sites and the people working in them. The spin-offs received supply contracts to cover the period over which they needed to find new customers. After that, they would be on their own, competing in this new and exciting world of contracting. This gave birth to the contract development and manufacturing organization. The spin-off facilities and people needed to feel their way along gradually, even nervously, as they learned the trade of finding business and working toward contracts.

Out goes clinical development

At approximately the same time as distribution and manufacture went, many of those involved in running clinical trials were lined up for the firing squad. Their work was regarded as routine, and Big Pharma companies handed them over to the contractor base, otherwise known as the people who used to work for them. The activities they had been undertaking at the mother ship involved monitoring patients on clinical trials, analyzing the data, liaising with regulators, carrying out biostatistical analysis, organizing supplies going to patients, checking out adverse events in the marketplace, and a range of other duties required of clinical development. The new entities were christened contract research organizations, and they also had to win business in order to survive and grow.

Products go too

Along with the people and facility assets, product assets also found their way onto the scrap heap. These were the ones that had outlived their patent lives, the products that earned all the healthy profits in the past. They were considered to be clogging up the sausage machines with products that didn't make the necessary returns, and so Big Pharma stopped making these products and left it to other companies to copy their products and service their once-loyal customers.

The copying companies—named generics—started turning Big Pharma leftovers into profitable businesses.

CHAPTER 4

New Business Models and Therapies Appear

Leavers and funders join forces

This mass divestment of assets resulted in the formation of business models that were not feasible when the Big Pharma companies owned the assets. The management teams in the new contractor base were under enormous pressure to survive beyond the initial contract period that their former employers gave them, typically five years. The search was on for new business, and this coincided nicely with newly "released" Big Pharma executives looking for opportunities and investors looking enviously at the returns that marketed drugs were providing for their owners. From this marriage made in heaven, biotech companies were conceived.

The idea behind biotechs appeared attractive. By assembling an executive team and a core staff of scientific and technical experts, the companies could complete all the activities of drug development without actually owning any of the "hardware." All a biotech needed was the purchase of the appropriate mix of clinical and nonclinical contractors to do the heavy lifting of drug development (File It). The cash to pay the contractors would come from the investors keen to make a return on their money.

This model was further extended into what became known as "virtual pharma," where the team of core experts was whittled down to a bare minimum, many of them comprising little more than ten or twenty people, often reliant on contractors to educate them in the niceties of drug development and the regulations. This was considered acceptable because their mission would be to move the process to the point where the compound could be sold to bigger companies, or the entire company purchased en bloc by a suitor with the necessary resources to move things on towards marketed products.

Generic companies pick up the scraps

The dropping of drugs when out of patent also resulted in new companies willing to work to much smaller margins by copying the original product that they had been prevented from doing under patent law. The Big Pharma companies seemed more than happy to abandon that piece of the market. These newly christened generic models did not have to go through the extensive clinical trials of patented drugs and therefore did not have to recover the costs of failures. The extent of the clinical research required of them was to prove that their copy was bioequivalent. That is, they had to prove the effect of the drug on the patient was equivalent (within an acceptable band) to the original drug. The regulators established the rules for the clinical trials required.

These companies received a welcome boost when the US Congress passed the Hatch-Waxman Act in 1984, actively encouraging the entry of generic into the market. The intention was to force down drug prices. Other countries, such as the United Kingdom, also made moves to ease the entry of generic, establishing requirements for generic substitution whenever possible. Generic companies supply the vast majority of prescription medicines sold around the world today.

Others pile in

As time has marched on, companies large, small, mini, and micro are now involved in developing and supplying medicines. As university spin-offs and start-ups have entered the fray, we now have an interesting mix of business models:

- Pharmaceutical innovator
- Biopharmaceutical innovator
- generic

27

- biosimilar
- biotech
- virtual
- speciality Pharma
- university spin-off
- start-up

The models deal in conditions ranging from mildly irritating to life threatening and terminal. To add to the models, we have breakthroughs in treatments of diseases.

Biologics lead the way to new therapies

In recent years, new classes of compounds have begun to emerge, namely biologics (or biologicals) and advanced therapy medicinal products. Biologics are made from living things using processes far more variable and complex than the traditional small-molecule products produced using chemistry (chemical synthesis). Their manufacture is also an order of magnitude trickier than making drugs based on chemistry alone. Even seemingly minor alterations in the process can change the product, with potentially devastating effect. This has led to the mantra in biologic Pharmaceuticals that "the process is the product." This draws a distinction with small-molecule compounds, where a particular molecule can be reproduced reasonably accurately independent of the facility and equipment used to make it. In biologics, the molecules are so large and complex that it is often impossible to define their molecular structures by analysis. All that is known is that a particular process has produced something that has a particular biological effect on a patient. Other manufacturers may not be able to replicate that product and its effect, even if the process appears to be exactly the same.

That is not the end of it. The sensitivity of biologics to temperature variation and other factors in the environment mean they can be lost in the blink of an eye. A moment's loss of concentration from an operator or material handler can mean months of work wasted. A temperature data logger not properly validated, activated, or downloaded can yield the same result: valuable product in the bin.

Even that is not the end of it. The potential for input materials to affect yield, potency, and quality of output can be dramatic, as the strength of each new supply of materials can vary widely depending on factors that are not always obvious to the receiving company. Getting to the truth with suppliers, especially when the upstream supply chain leads to seemingly anonymous donors, can be a nightmare and sometimes even impossible.

Even that is not the end of it. The costs of goods for biologics often make a promising compound commercially nonviable. The net result of all the factors is that a biologic is an order of magnitude more difficult to develop, supply, maintain safe and produce cost effectively than a small molecule product.

Advanced Therapy Medicinal Products arrive on the scene

Now we have come to the end of it, at least for the time being. A new generation of therapies based on the body's own biology—advanced therapy medicinal products—is on the rise. These products are similarly biologic in nature, with cell therapy, gene therapy, and tissue engineering. These use the body's own healing mechanisms and often target conditions associated with a patient's genetic makeup. The potential to cure disease is phenomenal, but it is still in its infancy. Almost all of the clinical trial work is in the very early stage and involves small numbers of patients in hospital settings.

There is also a subset of advanced therapy medicinal products—autologous cell therapy, which is specific to an individual patient. The patient's own cells are extracted, modified in some curative way, and then reintroduced into the body.

Rather than attempt to expand further with my limited scientific knowledge on the subject, we should hear from Dr. Drew Hope. Dr. Hope and I were both members of the Bioindustry Association's manufacturing advisory committee in the United Kingdom. His passion for making a difference in this brave new world of medicine

29

struck me immediately, and I always turn to him for wise words on this, his specialist subject.

An Expert Witness Statement: Dr. Drew Hope

Q. Dr. Hope, please briefly explain the state of play in the discovery field of advanced therapy medicinal products.

A. I have been working in the ATMP field for more than a decade and seen many changes, not least the emergence of success. One thing has been constant: a radical approach to drug discovery and development. It is hoped that patients with diseases that are currently unmet by conventional molecule-based medicines will benefit from ATMPs. These diseases are complex, and they need a complex cure.

Normal drug discovery selects through hits (using high-throughput screening to find random molecules that interact with a disease target) and leads (selected molecules that work and can be made into drugs) that undergo optimization. The ATMP approach is to engineer a biological solution: implant new brain cells to replace those lost in neurodegeneration, put in angiogenic cells to promote blood vessel growth if the arteries are blocked, genetically engineer immune cells to attack cancer markers. This approach presents a challenge because having designed and engineered your solution to the problem, there has been an absence of selection and testing before clinical trials start. The product is designed to do the job and satisfy the regulators, often by virtue of winning a one-horse race. This increases the risk that products come to market that do not meet the needs of the customer (the patient, not the regulator).

Q. So what are the challenges in the development of advanced therapy medicinal products?

A. Advanced therapies come in three flavors with increasing complexity: gene therapies, somatic-cell therapies, and tissue-engineered products. They are, obviously, biological and not chemical. This presents challenges. It is often difficult to fit a biological entity into a pharmaceutical/

health-care system that is designed for molecules. To illustrate this, try answering the question, "What is the active pharmaceutical ingredient in a bioengineered tracheal transplant?" One will need to know, because one will be writing how to make it and control it in one's clinical trial application or marketing dossier.

It is easier to think of advanced therapy medicinal products as a process of treatment rather than a drug that uses dosages. This example illustrates the challenge:

I work with autologous cell therapy projects in a large National Health Service hospital trust in London. The trust has a governance committee to review new drugs that might be used in the hospitals. At a meeting for one of my projects, the committee passed the review of an autologous cell therapy to another committee, which reviews the quality and risks associated with experimental treatment procedures. They thought, naturally, that they were ill equipped to review the treatment procedure and patient pathway. The second committee does not have the authority to review the use of new drugs in the hospitals. It is clear that advanced therapy medicinal products do not fit easily into this common health-care governance system, which will hinder progress toward widespread use.

Another challenge that makes advanced therapy medicinal products difficult to fit into the health-care system as drugs is that it can be difficult to know what it is about the product that provides efficacy and therefore is difficult to test their potency. Where I work, we are testing regulatory T-cell products in organ-transplant recipients. These products have been implicated in natural tolerance of transplanted organs in rare cases. It is rational to manipulate these cells to the patient's advantage using advanced therapy technology. We know of at least four ways that regulatory T-cells suppress immune responses. We do not know whether all four need to be working in our drug product for it to induce tolerance of the transplanted organ; or only three, but which three; or two, but which two. Do any of these methods cause side effects? We test one in a compromise, using a complicated cell-based analysis. This example is typical of cell therapies. No wonder Big Pharma has been reluctant to develop such poorly understood and complex drugs.

31

Another challenge for advanced therapy medicinal products is that they are viable biological systems that producers cannot put into an aluminium blister pack in a room-temperature warehouse for storage. The supply chain for these products requires a whole new set of technology, frequently including cryopreservation storage and transport solutions (liquid nitrogen at -196°C or-320° F), and short-shelf-life delivery systems so that doctors can administer the product even before it has been fully tested and certified. This will hinder many successful advanced therapy medicinal products from ever becoming blockbusters The scale of postmarketing rollout will be limited, and there are barely any hospital pharmacies with liquid-nitrogen freezers and even fewer keen to use them. My hope, and I am optimistic, is that new technology coupled with supply-chain logistics will rescue us. Nevertheless, I recognize that there will be some years until we see a type of cell therapy in an aluminium blister pack.

The final challenge is the adoption of proven advanced therapy medicinal products in a health-care system that is unfamiliar with them. Dendreon markets Provenge as a treatment of prostate cancer. It works well and can extend the lives of many patients. Being an autologous cell therapy, patients are obliged to visit a hospital for cell procurement (which is uncomfortable and time consuming), and then return three times over a course of some weeks for cell implantations. Patients have preferred familiar cancer drugs that have similar efficacy but are less of an ordeal and that they can take at home. Oncologists are not familiar with tissue or cell transplants and naturally prescribe molecules, preferring even new and unfamiliar molecules to cell transplants. Provenge has not met sales targets despite promising clinical data, resulting in lost jobs and the closures of manufacturing plants. Debt ridden, Dendreon has collapsed. The lesson advanced-therapy developers need to learn is to know the customer, and develop products that meet all of the customer's needs, and provide clinical efficacy.

ENDS

It is obvious from Dr. Hope's comments that advanced therapy medicinal products offer tremendous potential benefits to patients, but there are many unsolved issues in making these therapies available to patients. If we consider that this is an industry that is used to making one-size-fits-all products for global distribution and sale via third-party networks, the picture gets even more concerning. As we learned in the previous chapter, Pharma product license-holders and manufacturers have little, if any, contact with hospitals, community pharmacies, and patient care at home. If the industry is to respond to therapies that involve much smaller patient populations with specific needs, down to individual patients, even in home settings, how is it going to work?

The latest development is the advent of precision medicine, whereby doctors can make a diagnosis using technologies that can predict which therapy is required specific to a patient's genetic makeup and needs. This further magnifies the potential of alternative therapy medicinal products but has a similar magnification effect on the practical difficulties.

We will ponder this and revisit it later. In the meantime, we face disturbing news.

CHAPTER 5

Pharma Receives a SICCI-NING Diagnosis

The story so far is that of an industry riddled with conflicting messages about its state of well-being. After a comfortable lifestyle based on serendipitous discoveries and marketing muscle, Big Pharma has worrying signs that things are not what they should be. Life has become far more difficult than ever. Offers of help from all around are muddled and confused. How can the industry get to the bottom of things?

We will now dig into the summary for the Pharma industry to find out exactly what effect this has had, beginning with an excerpt from the final chapter of my previous book, Supply Chain Management in the Drug Industry: Delivering Patient Value for Pharmaceuticals and Biologics" to set the tone.

"The Pharmaceutical industry has always been fragmented, with no single company ever holding more than a single-digit market share. This fragmentation grew into full disconnectedness when Pharmaceutical companies began to retrench into the opposite ends of the business: discovery research and marketing. In metaphorical terms, the brain kept its head and legs and threw away its body, with arms attached. The body is now in no-man's land, making do as best it can with little meaningful contact with its previous fellow body parts.

"The head and legs are Pharmaceutical companies spearheading the drive to discover drugs to cure unmet medical needs and build a market for them. The disconnected body parts, the engine room of clinical and nonclinical development, manufacture, and supply, are sitting in the land of outsourced services. In this land it is survival of the fittest; and the fittest know how to manage commercial contracts for maximum benefit. There is also more to this disconnectedness. The marketing part of the head is not engaged with patients. The discovery research part of the head has now entered the disconnection game by outsourcing its work to small and medium-sized companies, known as biotech or virtual drug developers. These are typically companies with insufficient critical mass to undertake the vital early stage work required for modernization, discussed in earlier chapters."

ENDS

In that book, I coined the term SICCI to describe the condition this lifestyle has created. SICCI stands for *Serendipity Induced Chronic-disconnectedness, associated with Change Inertia.* It's a dreadful pun, I know, but it conveys a serious message. The companies that snapped up the assets that Big Pharma divested in the early days, grabbed and exploited them. It has left these Big Pharma companies as shadows of their former selves. Big Pharma is no longer big, not in relative terms.

Figure 6 shows the physical flow of materials required to make test material for a clinical trial. It also shows the data necessary to be submitted to regulators to prove that the drug is fit to market. The pharmaceutical company sponsoring the trial must supply all the information about the clinical, nonclinical, and manufacturing of its product to the regulator. If all is in order, the regulator awards the company a license to sell that product, subject to keeping everything in line with what was the license application promises. The information the regulator requires to consider the application has to be contained in a dossier, almost invariably of considerable size, and the company is responsible for putting it together. Collecting the information is a mammoth task, as I'm sure readers can imagine.

Compiling the dossier are hundreds, if not thousands, of people with multiple functional responsibilities across the many disciplines of drug development. The regulators almost invariably ask about the content of the dossier, and the same people might have to undertake a similar mammoth effort to provide the answers.

Before asset divestment, this task fell almost entirely under the company umbrella, and it was in everyone's interest to accomplish it. They would eventually share in the rewards of the hard labor required, either by growing their jobs, keeping their jobs, or even getting a little bonus or two.

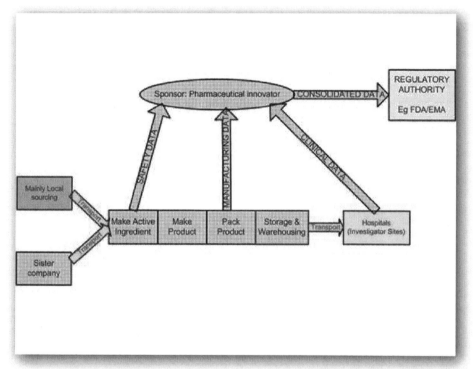

Figure 6. Making material for clinical trials, pre-asset divestment

When the Triple-F dynamic took over and the assets began to fly, the industry started on the road to disconnection. The SICCI virus had entered the bloodstream and was busily making a home for itself. This is what we have today, depicted in figure 7, after the virus has done its job.

We have Big Pharma companies retracting behind a wall of contractors yet still holding responsibility to the regulators to keep everything on track.

This chart is a much-simplified version because it couldn't possibly show the back and forth of materials, people, and information required to make this all work. A plethora of contractors is required to do most of the drudgery. Contract development and manufacturing organizations, contract research organizations, and third-party logistics providers, each one holding data that must go into the registration dossier. Most of the critical activity takes place in the contractors these days; notice the amount of Big Pharma owned resources that have disappeared from the

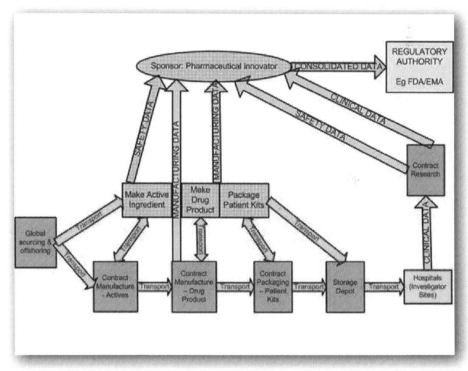

Figure 7. Making material for clinical trials, post-asset divestment

picture. Big Pharma is a shadow of its former self in terms of hands-on involvement. Further complicating the situation is the emergence of the different business models and the new therapy area, biologics. In Figure 8 below, we see that the minnows are in the game and biopharmaceutical companies are in the game.

There is now another wall between the Big Pharma company. The minnows are undertaking the preclinical and early-stage clinical trial work with the hope of selling to Big Pharma at some point. The further they go in the process, the more valuable their proposition becomes. This is where the speed dating mentioned earlier comes into play. Big Pharma companies have huge budgets and are looking for that elusive find. The minnows have small budgets and are looking for deals. Each is coy about what the other has in the hope that any showstoppers don't appear.

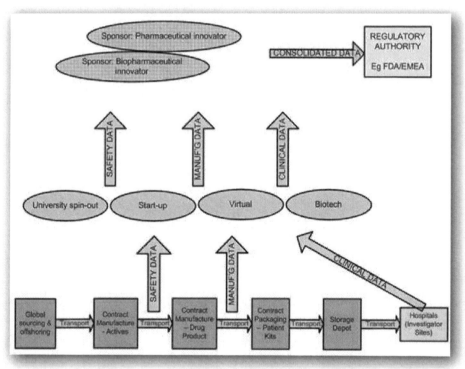

Figure 8. Minnows make material for clinical trials to sell-on to Big Pharma

This has led to a kind of feeding frenzy as deal-making conferences and events multiply and attract hundreds, if not thousands, to the world of pharmaceutical speed dating. Here, the Big Pharma suitors proudly display their bulging wallets while their prospective mates keep their skirts firmly around their assets beneath. Signatures of nondisclosure agreements seal the date, and courtship begins. Will this be a marriage made in heaven or hell? Only the gods know for sure.

The minnow business models show no intention of following through the process to market, needing to sell their wares on to one of the other business models looking toward market. We see from Figure 9 below the overall complexity and regulatory overload associated with the current situation as it stands today.

We have now been through the effects of SICCI on clinical trials and observed their increase in complexity. To date, the complexity has been

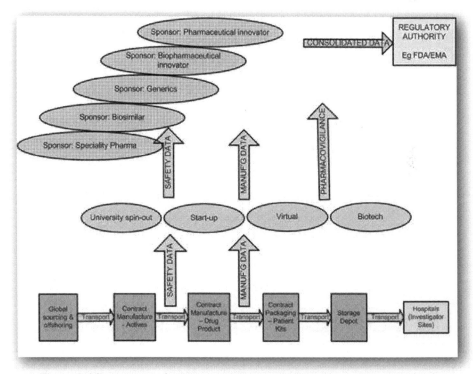

Figure 9. Minnows, new business models, complexity and regulatory overload

attributed to globalization of the supply chain. I hope you can see that even though market locations have globalized, it has been SICCI that causes the complexity and opportunity for things to go wrong in the various transfer points.

Having completed the analysis for clinical trials' supply chains, we can do a similar study of commercial supply chains. Bear in mind the massive differences in volume between commercial and clinical supply chains. My first book provides information to anyone interested in finding out more.

Figure 10 shows how things looked in the days before asset divestment.

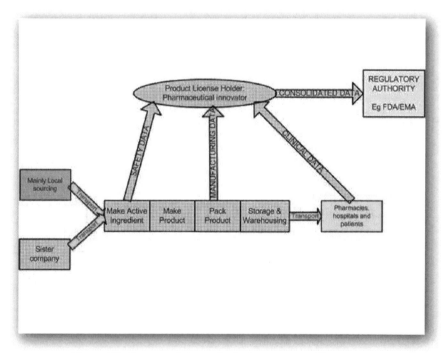

Figure 10. Commercial supply chains pre-asset divestment

The typical Big Pharma company would have ownership control over most, if not all, of the supply and production stages, up to the point where products were transported to their intended destinations, either local wholesaler networks or to hospitals and patients directly from their own warehouses.

Figure 11 depicts how it is today:

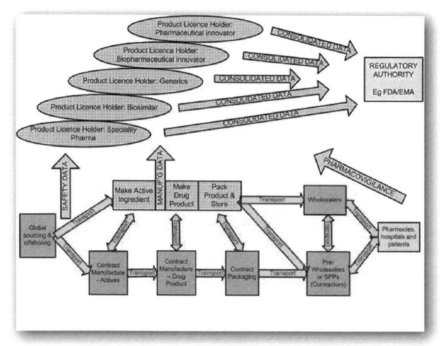

Figure 11. Commercial supply chains post-asset divestment with new business models

The tale of complexity is similar to clinical trials, only hundreds of times more challenging because these drugs will go to treat the world's population of patients in need of drugs. Pharma companies must have what are termed "pharmacovigilance" processes to detect any adverse events in the marketplace for their products. The outsourcing of "first response" to third parties makes this huge task by any stretch even more difficult.

We leave the complexity question for now and examine where all of this has left things.

Where has SICCI left things?

Disconnection from distribution and cash collection for finished products has resulted in three major Pharma distributors in the United States—AmerisourceBergen, McKessen, and Cardinal Health—holding roughly 80 percent of the market. In Europe, three major players— Celesio, Phoenix, and Walgreens Boots Alliance —account for the vast majority of movements from manufacturers to end users. These massive companies now are integrating further into the health-care system by acquiring or forging alliances with downstream operators dealing directly with patients and doctors.

As a result, the Big Pharma companies that own the licenses to sell the products have little or nothing to do with operations in the distribution network. They even have to pay specialist companies a lot of money to get access to their own sales data, which is normally well out of date when it arrives.

The contract development and manufacturing organisations have experienced similar dramatic growth. It is not difficult to find companies on the Internet that offer these services. Recurring names include Lonza, Catalent Pharma Solutions, Patheon, and Almac. You can look up these companies and others to see for yourself how professional these organizations have become. They also understand clearly how key they have become in developing and manufacturing drugs. There probably is not a drug-development company in the world that does not depend on one or more of these companies.

We have the same picture for contract research organizations. Well-known names are Quintiles, Parexel, and PPD. Within this clinical community, you can find any service under the sun to support your trials, such as study monitors, physicians, statisticians, data entry clerks, and medical directors. They can also help recruit the investigators responsible for the overall outcome of the trial and ensure payment as necessary.

Today, hardly anything hasn't been outsourced to some extent. Even for basic research, the Big Pharma companies seek to strike alliances with university spin-offs and biotech start-ups. The latest round of disconnection is outsourcing discovery research (Find It) to these "more nimble" organizations.

Then we have the out-of-patent products, the divestment of which has created a generics industry that has grown over the years. Teva, once a small company with headquarters in Israel, is now the biggest generic business in the world with a turnover of about twenty billion dollars followed by other companies of substantial size such as Sandoz (owned by Novartis), Mylan, and Actavis.

This is not the end of the disconnection. The various elements that make up diagnosis, therapy, and supportive care available to professionals and patients are disconnected. In Figure 12 below, the left-hand boxes are the manufacturers—Rx (prescription only), both patented and out of patent, diagnostics, medical devices, and various types of appliances and aids used in the medical setting. On the right-hand side are patients visiting their doctors and either having prescriptions to be filled by the community pharmacy or being referred to a hospital or specialist. The hospital will have its own pharmacy where patients can receive medication. To get to the pharmacy and then patients, all of the products have to go through the prewholesaler (third-party companies providing logistics services to Pharma in return for a fee) and wholesaler (logistics companies that buy products from the Pharma manufacturers and sell them on) networks.

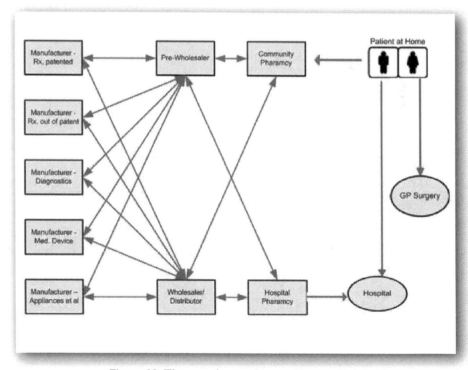

Figure 12. The complex product route to patients

The boxes on the left side give clues to what is going on. Many different companies, or different arms of the same companies, occupy the boxes. They may supply a patented prescription medicine but not an out-of-patent, diagnostic medical device, or appliance; or they may supply various combinations. The distribution networks are bombarded with products from a multitude of companies that go into the pot and eventually wind their way to waiting patients.

This is where we are today. We have an industry that has morphed from a mainly vertically integrated setup to the spaghetti model as illustrated above. Has this been good for the industry and the patients it serves? The following section will help us decide.

Part II Pharma Present

CHAPTER 6

PANIC AND CONFUSION REIGN IN THE INDUSTRY

Don't Panic, Captain Mainwaring!
Lance Corporal Jones, *Dad's Army*

We have not yet broken this SICCI-NING news to the industry. However, any patient with a condition has symptoms and
other signs that tell them things are not quite right. In this
chapter, we take a look at the underlying panic and confusion brought
about by that unspoken sense of doom.

For those not familiar with British television's *Dad's Army*, Lance
Corporal Jones was famous for cautioning all around not to panic while
exhibiting all the signs himself. He would brandish his bayonet and
declare, "They don't like it up 'em, you know" (the enemy, that is) and
implore his commanding officer, Captain Mainwaring, to set him loose
among them in a brave attempt to resolve the unfolding crisis. The captain always remained calm and berated Jones for his lack of self-control
and fortitude and took matters into his own hands.

Some say Big Pharma should be panicking, al la Corporal Jones, and
be ready to fix bayonets as we speak. Others are far more like the captain, refusing to be moved in the face of symptoms that might be worrying to some but mere figments of the imagination in reality.

Corporal Jones would point toward the many pundits in the
industry—prophets of doom, some might say—quoting a string of issues
such as eye-watering drug prices, dried-up product pipelines, patent

cliffs (with nothing to replace expiring product patents), generic competition (copycat drugs), tougher regulation (such as the FDA) and the valley of death (when drugs fail to get regulatory approval). The captain would caution against jumping to rash conclusions and look at the matter with a cool, calculating head. Accordingly, we take the captain's approach, ask the important questions on everyone's lips, and look for answers. We begin with the cost of developing a drug.

Does it cost a fortune to develop a drug?

Tuft's University declared in November 2014 that it cost $2.6 billion to develop a drug,[i] a 145 percent increase, correcting for inflation, over the estimate the center made in 2003. That is a very big number in anyone's book.

Shortly afterward, Medecins Sans Frontieres/Doctors Without Borders rebutted the report's findings.[ii] "if you believe that, you probably also believe the Earth is flat," the organization said. It quoted costs of around $50 million to develop certain drugs or up to $186 million if you took failure into account.

These are two very different assessments of the situation on the costs of drug development.

So who is right? Tuft's University? Medecins Sans Frontieres? Or is neither right and some other figure is the one to use?

There is no straight answer on this, and understandably so. It seems to depend on whom you ask.

Are some drugs too expensive?

In an article titled *Politicians Shouldn't Question Drug Costs But Rather Their Value. Lessons From Soliris And Sovaldi.*[iii] we hear the view of John L. LaMattina, PhD, former senior vice president of Pfizer Inc. and president of Pfizer global research and development. He comments:

---

i. http://cen.acs.org/articles/92/web/2014/11/Tufts-Study-Finds-Big-Rise.html

ii. http://www.doctorswithoutborders.org/article/rd-cost-estimates-msf-response-tufts-csdd-study-cost-develop-new-drug

iii. http://www.forbes.com/sites/johnlamattina/2014/08/04/politicians-shouldnt-question-drug-costs-but-rather-their-value-lessons-from-soliris-and-sovaldi/

"It is not too surprising to see politicians now suddenly jumping on the bandwagon and expressing outrage over the cost of new drugs. Sovaldi, a drug that essentially cures hepatitis C, has been the subject of numerous news stories focused on its cost—$84,000 for a twelve week course of treatment."

La Mattina argues that value, not cost, should be the yardstick. In the absence of transparency on how the cost is determined, though, it is impossible to make the balance of judgment on what is fair and whether politicians are jumping onto some kind of bandwagon as opposed to asking the questions that need to be asked.

Will drug prices become more transparent?

One of the issues in drug pricing now fervently discussed in the industry is the perception of secret discussions within companies that set the selling price. The Association of the British Pharmaceutical Industry has published the price and affordability of drugs and has reported, **"Pharma must engage on the affordability question, says ABPI:** UK Pharma trade body says the industry must be willing to discuss drug pricing"[iv]

The UK Pharma industry must stop talking about the affordability of drugs "behind closed doors" and be open to questions over medicine pricing.

This is according to Alison Clough, the acting chief executive of the ABPI, who told a conference in London in April 2015 that there had been much airtime devoted to the issue of drug affordability, which grew exponentially during the previous year.

She said Pharma has typically wanted to talk about this issue behind closed doors, "but now that changes," she said. "We need to find a solution to the question: how does society pay for medical progress?"

Clearly then, the UK industry body accepts that drug affordability is being called into question and the noise is growing rapidly. Even more positively, Clough seems to suggest that the industry should open its doors to discussion on drug pricing, although it's not obvious how that

---

iv. http://www.pmlive.com/Big Pharma_news/Big Pharma_must_engage_on_the_affordability_question,_says_abpi_718504

would work. The parting comment seems strange, though, as it is the "what" should society pay for medical progress that is being called into question rather than the "how." Presumably, the "how" would be some kind of check, banker's draft, or electronic money transfer.

Again, there is no conclusive version of events, which is disappointing, but on we go with our questions.

Is drug development really a risky business?

On this topic, we may be in luck because we can find hard evidence. In November 2006, the US Government Accountability Office issued a report titled *NEW DRUG DEVELOPMENT: Science, Business, Regulatory, and Intellectual Property Issues Cited as Hampering Drug Development Efforts.*[v] In Figure 13 below is a graphic that represents one of the key findings on the risk of failure.

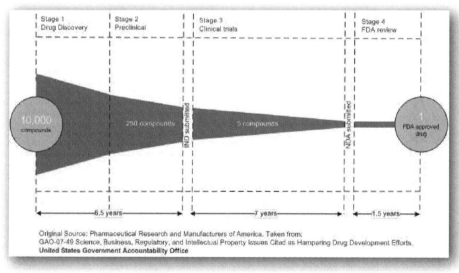

Figure 13 The risk of failure in drug development

The statistics speak for themselves. For every 250 compounds that enter the development pipeline, 249 fail to reach their destinations. Is

v. http://www.gao.gov/assets/260/253726.pdf

that risky enough for you? Apparently not, in the view of the ABPI-funded Office of Health Economics. The director, Professor Adrian Towse, during the same conference as Alison Clough, noted that only 11 percent of drugs that begin testing in the first phase would be expected to make it to approval. "In essence, we are paying for failure," Towse said, but added that this was simply a result of taking on more risk.

I've read this last paragraph over and over again and still can't rationalize the use of the word "simply," given what we now know of the horrendous failure rates in drug development. At least, though, we can draw a conclusion that drug development is a risky business and it is getting riskier.

Is Big Pharma becoming more focused on the patient these days?

There is much talk these days about Big Pharmaceutical companies becoming centered on the patient, and US legislation is demanding it. The US government's "21st Century Cures Act,"[vi] Title II: Patient-Focused Drug Development, calls for greater consultation and involvement of patients in the development of drugs. There seems to be a long way to go, however. In his article *Developing your patient-centric strategy*[vii] Richard Jones, managing director of Open Health's patient engagement agency, makes the following points:

"As a concept 'patient-centricity'—the process of designing a service or solution around the patient—is really rather simple, but as an aim for pharmaceutical companies it is all too often overlooked.

"Yet there is no denying the increasing buzz around being patient-centric and close to the patient. Here in the UK it has been driven by NHS thinking like 'no decision about me, without me,' and ideas around putting the patient at the heart of decision-making and discussions have taken root in many countries.

---

vi. https://www.congress.gov/bill/114th-congress/house-bill/6/text
vii. http://www.pmlive.com/Big Pharma_news/developing_your_patient-centric_strategy_557457

"Within the industry companies often express their desire to be patient-centric organizations. Whether 'inspired by patients, driven by science' (UCB); 'science and patients...the heart of everything we do' (AstraZeneca); or being 'a global integrated healthcare leader focused on patients' needs' (Sanofi), the industry has enthusiastically grasped the idea of patient-centricity.

"But companies such as UCB, AstraZeneca and Sanofi, like the rest of the industry, have brands and brand managers. So Big Pharma's challenge is how to be truly patient-centric when your vehicle of engagement is a brand, not a disease."

ENDS

Richard makes an excellent point, and we will return to this concern over brands, not patients, later.

Investigating the question further, an excerpt from an article in the United Kingdom's Daily Mail, Tuesday, July 7, 2015, had this to say about Pharmas attitude toward patient need:

"From simple white paracetamol to blue diamond-shaped Viagra, our pills come in all shapes, sizes, and colors."

The conclusion from the article is that the industry does not take account of the patient need because it doesn't have to. There are no specific rules it needs to follow.

We could determine from the above then, that patient-centricity has not been a concern in the past, but there is pressure from outside to move that way.

Is there a lack of innovation in drug development?

PhRMA, the Pharmaceutical Research and Manufacturers of America, counters any argument that Big Pharma lacks innovation. This is what the industry body has to say on the topic:[viii]

---

viii. http://www.phrma.org/innovation

"As one of the most research-intensive and science-driven industries in the US, the Pharmaceutical industry is committed to the research and development (R&D) of new treatments and cures for patients, including those who have serious unmet medical needs. With more than 7,000 innovative drugs in development worldwide by Pharmaceutical companies and over $500 billion invested in R&D since 2000, hope is certainly on the horizon."

At the same time, there are mounting complaints from a number of quarters about "me-too" drugs. These are drugs that are approved for sale even though they are no better than the ones already on the market. One of our expert witnesses, Jack Shapiro, president of JM Shapiro Healthcare Marketing Research and Management Consulting in Maywood, NJ, had this to say:

"Too many of our drugs are basically expensive me-too drugs that offer minimal, if any, advantages over earlier compounds. Physicians know this, and patients eventually figure it out and can't understand why their doctor is making them pay so much for so little. High-tier copays don't help this problem."

ENDS

Who is right on this one? There appear to be thousands of drugs under development but a shortage of evidence on how many get through to make a difference in the lives of patients. Could there be some confusion in the industry over what innovation is really all about?

Is Big Pharma too sales driven?

For an inside track on this question, we turn to an expert witness, Hanno Wolfram. I came across an article of his in PharmaPhorum on the topic of patient-centricity and was impressed by his insights. He has extensive experience of sales and marketing in the industry, and I asked him to share his experiences of selling in Pharma.

AN EXPERT WITNESS STATEMENT: MR. HANNO WOLFRAM

Q. How did Big Pharma sales-field forces operate prior to the block-buster era?

A. In the early days of pharmaceutical field forces, those employees visiting and consulting physicians on therapeutic issues were called "medical representatives." Their task was to represent their company's expertise concerning the treatment of specific diseases. In these early days, medical representatives had a very clear mission statement: "No one knows more about therapy than we do."

Physicians had their doors wide open, and more often than not, medical representatives were welcomed with the sentence: "Dear colleague, do you prefer coffee or tea?" Calls lasted fifteen to thirty minutes on average. The objective of that visit was simple: to answer any question a physician had. Doctors discussed their problems in scientific depth and breadth with their "therapeutic advisors."

Medical representatives those days fully respected that symptom assessment and diagnosis were solely and fully the clinician's domain. Finding a diagnosis was even called the art of a medical doctor. Yet vast knowledge about therapy and the ability to advise and consult physicians on the right drug to prescribe was a domain of well-trained and perfectly equipped medical representatives. If there was any kind of flu, bacterial, or viral endemic, medical representatives gathered experiences and shared them with all of their doctors. Scientific literature and the latest publications in renowned magazines were always part of valued and valuable discussions. It was absolutely clear that, once asked, they proposed the optimal therapy. It was not at all mandatory, nor expected, that they only and always suggested "their drug" as the best option.

In those days, physicians trusted medical representatives and were seen as next of kin. Physicians were easily accessible, and medical representatives were their sources of in-depth therapeutic knowledge. Medical representatives' visits were welcome interruptions of the daily routine of asking and listening to patients. The medical representative who came, then, was the welcome listener. Clinicians could speak out, ask questions, and share everyday details at a professional eye level. Asking for advice from a trusted person in a confidential setting was what made medical representatives irreplaceable for many physicians—in those bygone days.

Q. What changes did you observe in Big Pharma's selling practices?

A. Big Pharma changed strategy and started to hire salespeople for their field forces. Someone had come up with the idea that "selling" delivered more than helping physicians make the best therapeutic choices, consult, advise, and share the huge pharma disease know-how with prescribers.

After "selling" as a technical term had been established, the era of the "race of arms" started. The more representatives you had, the faster you could achieve market penetration. The dose-response curve had been copied from the research people. Consultants called it the "S-curve." The more calls in a certain time, in the shortest possible frequency per physician, the higher the revenue, until the "S" flattened out to a point of diminishing return.

From fast-moving consumer goods companies, Big Pharma learned the utmost importance of "knowing thy customer." This finding included the introduction of the word "customer." Today, almost every touch-point pharma might have, is named "customer." After the term "customer" was widely used, customer relationship management was born. Today, customer relationship management has widely degenerated to a policing tool of a representative's activities and prerequisite for analysis, often showing little practical or managerial relevance.

This selling vocabulary for Big Pharma coined a mentality and led to laws and codes of conduct—and simultaneously Pharma's ideas to circumvent them. A number of anticorruption laws originate from Pharma's "selling skills," especially from the step called "closing the deal." Growing sales became the core objective and key performance indicator in Pharma. Yet being sales driven started to result in legal trials, prison sentences, and billion dollar-fines.

After these painful selling attempts, the majority of the target group today says: "No there is no value seeing a Pharma salesperson." More and more access restrictions are subsequently imposed. In some countries, more than 50 percent of all prescribers have fully closed their doors to Pharma.

ENDS

We learn here from Wolfram of a rapid rise in the sales mentality within Pharma, aimed at selling to prescribing doctors, and the metrics that drive the need to sell.

Does the industry turn a blind eye to side effects?

An article in the UK Telegraph,[ix] by Laura Donnelly and Edward Malnick reported on the United Kingdom's National Health Service's advice that there should be widespread use of statins:

> "The advice has divided experts, with prominent doctors accusing NICE's (National Institute for Health and Care Excellence) experts of being too close to the Pharmaceutical industry."

Debate has raged for some time over the risks and benefits of taking a statin every day. The proponents of statins argue that lower cholesterol levels serve to reduce the overall risk of heart problems in the over 55's population, whereas the opponents do not accept patients should be exposed to the potential side effects unless there is a properly diagnosed need.

One general practitioner describes the side effects as "horrific," and a large percentage refuse to follow the advice, even though they could be financially penalized by not following NICE's dictate.

Aside from the statin debate, the industry has a less-than-stellar record for being truthful about safety profiles of drugs, as evidenced by Vioxx, which has left a bitter taste in the mouths of many families and doctors affected. For those not familiar with the story, Merck gained US FDA approval to launch a painkiller Vioxx (rofecoxib), in 1999, based upon clinical trial evidence.

Following launch, there emerged a growing body of evidence that the drug was implicated in heart attacks and death. The Drugwatch site[x]

---

ix. http://www.telegraph.co.uk/news/health/news/11201669/GPs-refusing-to-prescribe-statins.html

x. http://www.drugwatch.com/vioxx/recall/

reported "In the years that followed, it was mired in scandal. Merck was accused of misleading doctors and patients about the drug's safety, fabricating study results to suit the company's needs, continually thwarting an FDA scientist from revealing the drug's problems and skirting federal drug regulations." During this time, patients were dying.

Campaigns have been started to achieve far greater visibility of safety profiles and other critical issues involved in clinical trials. In his book *Bad Pharma*[xi], physician Ben Goldacre reveals astonishing insights into the workings of the industry.

None of this, however, seems to be persuading the industry to change.

Are copycat drugs (generics) the same as the original?

I start again with an expert witness, Richard Meyer, a LinkedIn member of my discussion group Friends of Modernization in the Drug Industry. He is also a prolific writer about the industry, particularly with respect to marketing practices.

Meyer will pitch in here with a snippet from one of his frequent reports on industry issues.[xii]

Q. Tell us a little bit about concerns that generic drugs are not the same as originals.

A. I had the chance yesterday to be on the *Huffington Post Live* to discuss generic drugs in wake of the article by Fortune on Ranbaxy. Not surprisingly a lot of people chimed in and had concerns about generic drugs, which is no surprise considering that the FDA's definition of bioequivalence is surprisingly broad: A generic's maximum concentration of active ingredient in the blood must not fall more than 20 percent below or 25 percent above that of the brand name. This means a potential range of 45 percent by that measure, among generics labeled as being the same.

---

xi. Goldacre, Ben, *Bad Pharma*, Fourth Estate, 2012, updated 2013

xii. http://worldofdtcmarketing.com/are-generics-really-equal-to-branded-drugs/cost-of-healthcare-in-the-u-s/

There are other differences. The generic must contain the same active ingredient as the original. But the additional ingredients, known as excipients, can be different and are often of lower quality. Those differences can affect what's called bioavailability—the amount of drug that could potentially be absorbed into the bloodstream. As the American Heart Association recently noted, "Some additives traditionally thought to be inert, such as alcohol sugars, cyclodextrans, and polysorbate-80, may alter a drug's dissolution, thereby impacting its bioavailability."

The FDA standards also do not specifically regulate how quickly the medicine reaches peak concentration in the blood. That can become a major issue for patients who take generic versions of time-release drugs, which constitute 10 percent of the market, according to IMS Health. The time-release mechanisms for branded drugs are usually protected by separate patents, so generics companies engineer alternative and usually cheaper mechanisms.

That can result in drugs that release active ingredients into the blood far more quickly, leaving patients feeling dizzy or nauseated. Barbara Davit, director of the division of bioequivalence II in the FDA's Office of Generic Drugs, acknowledges that the agency does not apply "formal statistics" to measuring Tmax, the time it takes for a drug to reach maximum concentration. But reviewers do informally consider it, she says, asserting that applications have been rejected because of Tmax results.

Q; Interesting Richard. What do you think empowered patients are going to think about this information? Are they going to believe it, or are they going to see a sinister conspiracy by the drug industry to throw mud on generic drugs?

A: I worked in the generic drug industry for over-the-counter products and can tell you that there are differences between branded drugs and generics. Are those differences worth an 85 percent price premium? Probably not, but drug companies would be smart to lower prices of branded drugs significantly when their product comes off patent. Physicians should also listen to patient complaints about side effects after they have been switched to generics and to monitor outcomes of generics versus branded drugs.

ENDS

Meyer explains why generics are not always the same as the original product.

There is also further evidence from FiercePharma's web report titled *fda-quietly-testing-some-drugs-generic-equivalency*,[xiii] which states, "An independent study of generic versions of Pfizer's cholesterol-lowering drug Lipitor, done by Preston Mason at Brigham & Women's Hospital, found some of the generics were ineffective because of impurities resulting from the manufacturing."

ENDS

This is a topic that interests me, as I go on to explore.

VIEWS, OBSERVATIONS, AND PERSONAL EXPERIENCES OF THE AUTHOR

I have been told by some of the world's greatest authorities on the manufacture of drugs, during discussions in my Friends of Modernization in the Drug Industry LinkedIn group, that the nonactive ingredients (excipients) that go into making the tablet or other dosage form can seriously affect the performance of the drug. Not all, but there are some well-known cases where this has happened and probably others that have not come to light. I am told that the testing of a generic, to prove equivalence with the original Pharma product, does not identify these differences. To me, that is a big issue because patients tend to be unaware of this and there is so much pressure to move patients toward generic versions to save costs.

There is also an irony in that the drug development approval process does not allow the generic company access to nonactive ingredients in the original formula and as we learned above, these can have an important effect on a drug's performance.

---

xiii. http://www.fiercepharma.com/story/fda-quietly-testing-some-drugs-generic-equivalency/2014-02-24

59

ENDS

We move on now to another high-profile question.

Animal testing

The BBC reported[xiv] on June 4, 2015, the European Union's decision to declare that it was not possible to develop drugs without testing in animals. During the debate leading up to the decision, the British trade body had this to say:

> "While the UK's bio-Pharmaceutical industry says it is committed to reducing and ultimately replacing the use of animals for scientific research, 'this is not yet possible due to the complexity of the interactions between cells, tissues, and organs in the body, which cannot yet be fully modeled in vitro or by computers,' Dr Virginia Acha, ABPI executive director for Research Medical and Innovation told CNBC[xv] via e-mail."

On the other hand, Stop Vivisection, the group responsible for the petition, argues that animal testing has hindered development of alternative biomedical research methods and poses a danger to human health and the environment. On its website,[xvi] the organization says that existing provisions allow for testing on stray cats and dogs.

More conflicting opinions prevent us from drawing a conclusion. We finish here with my own specialty subject, the end-to-end pharmaceutical supply chain.

What is going on in the Pharma supply chain?

Many from outside the industry and more from inside are unfamiliar with operations in the Pharma supply chain in recent years. These

---

xiv. http://www.bbc.co.uk/news/world-europe-3301546

xv. http://www.cnbc.com/id/102667554

xvi. http://speakingofresearch.com/2015/06/03/european-commission-rejects-stop-vivisection-initiative/

typically appear under the categories of economically motivated adulteration, shortages, counterfeiting, and cargo diversion/theft.

Economically motivated adulteration first hit the news in 2007 when a toxic ingredient was found in Heparin (a blood-thinning agent) supplied by Baxter. It resulted in reports of 574 adverse events, nine patient deaths and hundreds injured. Investigators discovered that Baxter had procured raw materials from a rogue source. The source saved costs by using what turned out to be a toxic substance. Suddenly, economically motivated adulteration was a term on everyone's lips. After the incident, Pew Charitable Trust released an excellent, in-depth report titled *After Heparin.*[xvii]

This is the summary of the situation from Pew:

"In late 2007, US health officials began receiving reports of unexpected allergic-type reactions in patients undergoing dialysis. The reactions were linked to a widely used blood thinner—heparin—and specifically to an adulterant that had been introduced during manufacture of the drug in China. The US Food and Drug Administration (FDA) believes the adulteration of heparin was an economically motivated act—a clear breach of the US pharmaceutical supply chain.

"Pharmaceutical manufacturers and distributors work together in a robust system to deliver high-quality products, but drug manufacturing and distribution have become increasingly complex in recent years. Prescription and over-the-counter (OTC) medications originate in factories all over the world, moving into the American marketplace through supply chains that can involve numerous processing plants, manufacturers, suppliers, brokers, packagers, and distributors.

"The number of drug products made outside of the United States doubled from 2001 to 2008, according to FDA estimates. The FDA estimates that up to 40 percent of finished drugs used by US patients are manufactured abroad, and 80 percent of

xvii. http://www.pewtrusts.org/en/research-and-analysis/reports/2011/07/12/after-heparin-protecting-consumers-from-the-risks-of-substandard-and-counterfeit-drugs

active ingredients and bulk chemicals used in US drugs come from foreign countries. Increasingly, the United States relies on drug manufacturing in developing countries—mainly China and India. Globalization, increased outsourcing of manufacturing, the complexity of pharmaceutical distribution, and the existence of criminal actors willing to capitalize on supply chain weaknesses has created the potential for counterfeit or substandard medicines to enter the system and reach patients. As evidenced by the adulteration of heparin and other case studies outlined in this report, these rare but potentially serious events can have grave consequences."

ENDS

Product shortages in the supply chain attracted the attention of the US government, and on October 31, 2011, President Barack Obama signed an executive order directing the Food and Drug Administration to take action to reduce prescription-drug shortages, which the White House said had endangered patients and led to price gouging. He explained the reason for the order.

"Recently, we have seen how the potential of drug shortages for vital drugs, including some cancers, can really have an adverse impact on patients and those who are caring for patients. Sometimes we run out of or run low on certain types of drugs, and that drives up prices and it increases patient risk," President Obama said at the signing in the Oval Office.

"The executive order instructs the FDA to take action in three areas: broaden reporting of potential drug shortages, expedite regulatory reviews that can help prevent shortages, and examine whether potential shortages have led to illegal price gouging.

"Over the last five years, the number of these drug shortages has nearly tripled. Even though the FDA has prevented an actual crisis, this is one of those-slow rolling problems that could end up resulting in disaster for patients and health-care facilities all across the country. Congress has been trying since February to do something about this. It has not yet been able to get it done, and it is the belief of this administration...that we can't wait for action on the Hill. We've got to go ahead and move forward."

ENDS

We see here that concern over supply-chain issues moved even the US president into action. For deep insight into was has been going on, we turn to an expert witness, Catherine Geyman.

I met Geyman through her connection with Core Risks, a US-based supply-chain risk management company. Her deep understanding of the industry and the vulnerability of Pharma supply chains were refreshing, as was her company's ability to provide means to manage that risk. This is what she has to say on the matter:

AN EXPERT WITNESS STATEMENT: CATHERINE GEYMAN

Q. What do you make of the shortages issue?

A. The (lack of) resilience of global pharmaceutical supply chain networks has been laid bare in recent years by the global drug shortage crisis mentioned above, which peaked in 2011. As with any systemic supply-chain issue, the causes are numerous and complex, but they tend to hub around self-imposed cost-reduction initiatives removing the historical slack in supply chain's ability to absorb the impact of quality deviations. This increasing pressure in the industry to become more cost effective has led to initiatives such as blanket safety stock reduction, removing any slack in the supply chain.

In some cases, stock is there for a very good reason: to mitigate a significant single-source dependency or protect a product launch from forecast uncertainties. When taken away, it can result in severe issues in response to unplanned events.

Q. What other effects have you seen from cost-reduction efforts?

A. A company's asset base may also have suffered from the sharpening of the accountant's pencil. The removal of redundant capacity can also result in disruption being felt in the marketplace. Also, outsourcing to countries with immature regulatory regimes is another manifestation of the cost-reduction drive. The unhappy side effect of this has been the accompanying decrease in quality standards.

Separate European and US Drug root cause analyses of the acute drug shortages were carried out in 2011/12, and the general consensus was that quality problems were the biggest contributors to the shortages. Unsurprisingly, the "low cost" suppliers that can demonstrate superior quality standards have attracted the large customers, and the net result is a concentration of risk on certain contract manufacturers. This leaves a proportion of the industry vulnerable not only to the ongoing viability of certain suppliers, but in some cases exposed to the increased threat of natural hazards and political instabilities that are part of the package.

Q. Who else has had a part to play in this?

A. The regulators have also played their part in both the problem and the solution. Regulatory interventions were a contributory factor to the acute shortages of 2011–12 when a number of major manufacturers voluntarily shut down to correct systemic quality failings and the marketplace simply didn't have the capacity to fill the gap. However, following some high-profile finger pointing, the regulators are playing a much more positive role in resolving drug shortages by not enforcing recalls of certain drugs that were already in short supply, fast-tracking new products, and allowing products in from other markets.

Q. Has industry consolidation played a part?

A. The industry's manufacturing base is being consolidated through takeover. Mergers and acquisitions inevitably result in rationalization of assets in particular where the merging companies were previously selling substantially similar products. The net result is a global marketplace with fewer sourcing options.

Q. What risks do you see that remain lurking in Pharma supply chains?

A. By way of example of the range of risks and issues facing the Pharma supply base:

- Tight margins rule the chemical, food, and widget suppliers, making them particularly susceptible to the economic cycle. The 2008 economic crisis saw key Pharma polymer suppliers hit financially (particularly by the downturn in the automotive industry), resulting in idling of plants and a reduction in the already constrained supply base. Furthermore, Pharma companies often present an unattractive prospect with their low volume requirements and exacting specifications, making relationship building to mitigate the risks a challenge.

- Certain biologics products that depend on living things as a fundamental feedstock can also be a cause for many a supply chain manager's sleepless nights. While the originators of specific cells such as cattle are closely controlled and often isolated from the food supply chain, they are nonetheless vulnerable to infectious disease and even to benign cell contamination that can manifest itself quietly during development and only rear its ugly head postcommercialization.

- Specialist delivery device manufacturers are often unique, sole sources and very difficult to replace. It's not only the exacting specification of a device or material that can make finding an alternative challenging; it is also necessary that the downstream validation (evidence that the manufacturer can achieve the required standard) batches can make the time to establish an alternative months rather than weeks.

- This leads onto some of the limitations that the industry has been known to place on itself such as naming a specific supplier or a particular supplier's grade of material in the regulatory dossier, making the prospect of changing suppliers or establishing

65

alternatives in an emergency a potentially time-consuming process.

- The industry also has a fundamental fear of the regulator and consequently any changes/improvements to a validated process tend to be few and far between. This also has implications for finding alternative sources of supply should things go wrong, which makes recovering from any supply chain disruptions a lengthy process.

ENDS

This is confirmation, then, that the pursuit of short-term cost savings in the supply chain has had drastic implications for the industry; also, that it is not out of the woods yet.

Similar issues have been taking place in the European Union, albeit the finished product shortage issue had its roots in a different dynamic than the United States. This was driven largely by what is known as parallel trade. Drugs that have been bought by an intermediary in a lower-price EU country, repackaged in the new language and then resold in the higher-price EU market. It resulted in those buying products from the pharmaceutical manufacturers, such as pharmacies and even hospitals, ordering above their needs from the manufacturers to sell on to the repackagers and make a better return than they were getting from the health-care system in their own country. Unlike the United States, there has been no opportunity to legislate because the practice is legal under EU competition laws and, in fact, the parallel traders are awarded licenses to do it.

Counterfeit medicines have also found their way into the legitimate supply chain for pharmaceutical products, with the potential to harm, maim, and kill patients. Here are just two examples:

- As of March 31, 2014, counterfeits of Pfizer's medicines have been found in 107 countries and breached the legitimate supply chain in sixty countries.
- In April 2014, falsified vials of the breast cancer treatment Herceptin were found in Europe after Herceptin vials had been stolen in Italy and undergone tampering.

In 2011, the European Union passed the Falsified Medicines Directive, leading to major revisions to the laws of good distribution practice and some revisions to good manufacturing practice, including a requirement for track-and-trace on certain higher-risk finished products. In the United States, the FDA Safety and Innovation Act became law, again with the intention of cracking down on illicit activities in the supply chain, as well as encouraging better working practices. More recently, the FDA has penned the Drug Supply Chain Security Act. Similarly to the European Union, it calls for track-and-trace to be implemented, albeit to a less-challenging timetable than the European Union.

Where does all this panic and confusion leave us?

The short answer is that it is impossible to tell what this all means, because whom do you believe? This has traditionally been an industry shrouded in mystery, and those who should know are either keeping to themselves unintentionally or withholding the truth on purpose. For the sake of convenience, I am going to coin an all-embracing term for those contributing to the panic and confusion: The Establishment.

Because the aim of this book is to get to the truth of the matter and the Morgan family has been helpful, we visit them again for inspiration.

A Helpful Metaphor

Morgan Morgan returned to the farmhouse dinner table with a grim look on his face.

"What was that all about?" Morfydd inquired.

"It was Mr. Evans-Bevan, woman. Who else do you think it was?"

"What did he say?" Morfydd asked tentatively.

"Oh, the usual. He wanted to know where we are with the new succulent sausages on the go. He's getting a lot of heat from his people at the bank."

Morfydd pressed her luck further with Morgan's anger. "Did you tell him what had happened to the latest range we sent for sampling?"

"Of course I didn't. Do you think I'm mad, woman? He'd go ballistic if he knew they didn't go down well with the samplers. We just need more time to come up with some answers."

Dafydd knew his mother could venture no further. He decided to continue with the questioning himself.

"What is happening though, Dad? Are we losing our touch, or is something else going on?"

Morgan took a more conciliatory tone with his only son.

"I'm as baffled as you are, Dafydd. We seem to be doing all the same things we did in the early days, just the succulent sausages aren't coming through."

Dafydd looked thoughtfully at his father and asked the first of a number of questions that had been bothering him for some time.

"Do you think we were right to sell off the sausage machines, Dad?"

"I know what you mean, son. Since they have been contracting to us, they seem to have stopped trying. Each time we want to develop a new sausage, the first question is how much will we pay to develop it? We can't do it on our own anymore, and they know that. If no sausages come out at the end, it's no skin off their nose."

Neither was in the mood to laugh at the unintended pun, and Morfydd didn't dare.

Dafydd inquired further.

"Why didn't we keep making the sausages when the queen's special period ran out? The companies making copies of our old ones seem to be doing wonderful trade, and all are making good profits."

"I know, I know, Dafydd. Don't you think I haven't thought about that?"

Then Dafydd asked, "What about all these small guys that have sprung up and are offering to sell us part finished sausages they claim to be succulent, using our former sausage machines to do it. When we've bought them, they didn't fit properly into the sausage machine we use and the data was not as good as they said. The other thing, Dad, these days it's costing us a king's ransom to keep the queen and her subjects on board with our sausages and hold the competition out."

"We're in a different ball game now, Dafydd. They are finding more and more different types of aversion to the vegetarian diet that needs a protein supplement, and there's our opportunity if you ask me. If we can find a cure for some of these rare conditions, we can be in a position to make a lot of money again. True, they are a lot pickier about cows getting tummy upsets, and the same with the rest of the sampling system, but if we keep throwing pork at it, we're sure to get there in the end, aren't we?"

Dafydd, still not convinced, made the next point.

"Along with this, we are struggling to get the attention of all these contractors. They have lots of new clients now developing sausages of their own. We have to pay them a lot of money to work on our trials and make the sausages for us. And they don't always know exactly what we are looking for. We have to keep everything secret from them in case they start making our sausages themselves. Do you really think we can go on like this, Dad?"

"'I don't know' is the simple answer, Dafydd, but I can't see what else we can do other than keep plugging away at it."

Dafydd nodded thoughtfully and said, "We've got to see a proper consultant on this, Dad, one who knows what he's talking about, and I think I know who that is."

CHAPTER 7

HARSH REALITIES FOR BIG PHARMA
AND THE INDUSTRY UNEARTHED

W ithout further ado, we get to the overarching harsh reality with the aid of another metaphor.

A Helpful Metaphor

Big Pharma was crippled by a debilitating addiction many years ago. As with any addiction, lifestyle choices are at the center of the problem. For the addictive gambler, the roots of their demise lie in early success. Seduced by the rush of easy money, it becomes a way of life. The gambler doesn't feel the need to go out and work, preferring instead to focus on beating the odds. Nothing is as important as the next win, and possessions and relationships often are discarded in order to fuel the habit. By the time the gambler realizes the problem, it is all too late: no home, no family, and few friends, little money, and no prospect of being able to hold down a job.

ENDS

In terms of the metaphor, the Triple F lifestyle yielded megareturns in the early days. The bank of molecule "chips" was duly replenished and systematically placed on the roulette wheel of regulatory review, waiting for that fateful black ball to drop, hopefully resulting in an approval from the regulators and megareturns.

When the odds began to go against it, facilities and people were cast out to conserve the stash in the bank. As the odds continued to favor the house, resources were funneled into FIND IT and FLOG IT. FILE IT increasingly became the poor relation, taken for granted as the necessary evil to be overcome on the road to life in the sun.

This, of course, has been the fatal mistake. FILE IT covers the entire product-development cycle, from conceptualization to commercialization. The early successes in Pharma struck the industry blind to the true nature of what it was doing. The industry is still blind to it. That is why this is the overriding harsh reality. The industry and Big Pharma, in particular, is an addict in denial, still placing its bets on the regulatory roulette wheel.

This may seem an extreme assessment, and in some ways it is because Big Pharma companies are still relatively rich. However, the industry's key players do exhibit many of the characteristics of the gambler: an obsession with chasing the big win (blockbusters); low-level engagement in key relationships (for example, patients, doctors, contractors, regulators, and distributors); divestment of life possessions to fund the stake and hedge the uncertainty (mass, tactical outsourcing, and abandonment of out-of-patent products); and a mind-set embedded in those early years of success, as an alternative to the hard yards of working for a living.

If we take the metaphor at face value, things don't look good for Big Pharma companies, as habits of a lifetime die hard. Often, addiction is a slow downward spiral into the gutter. Some would argue that is the trajectory before us, the logical conclusion of a lifetime of neglect. It would be perfectly reasonable to see it that way, given what we now know.

If the addict were to accept its plight, acknowledge the problem, and seek rehabilitation, there would be further harsh realities to face that stem from the lifetime of addiction. These need to be unearthed to appreciate the scope of the journey ahead, if it is to be one of recovery. We explore them in the remainder of this chapter.

Big Pharma needs a science lesson

Science is at the core of the industry—the lion's roar. On that front is a two-part lesson.

71

First, in the commercial world, science is impotent if not partnered with the translational methods in the world of engineering. Together, they travel from a good idea to a product in the hands of end users.

Second, far too little science is applied in the early stage of FILE IT. I will explain more because I suspect industry stalwarts will be up in arms at this point.

Observations, Views, and Experiences of the Author

Important though science is in any endeavor, we don't dwell on the physics or thermodynamics involved in flight, nor the science of the internal combustion engine, nor any other product that ends up on the market. We know it must have been there, but that's it. "Ah, but the human body is a million times more complex than an aircraft or a car." they declare. "Medicine is different."

Yes to the first point, no to the second. Making medicine is no different. There is so much we don't understand about the sky, yet we make aircraft, rockets, and satellites by accepting the unknowns and working around them. Whether the sky is less complex than the human body, who knows? That is academic. Humans will probably never understand either.

Developing medicines for humans is no different. Yes, there is science in deciding what molecular structures could target particular disease mechanisms and receptors, but the dreadful attrition rates tell us this is something of a blunt instrument. Remember, 249 out of 250 scientific theories were wrong, and it took years to discover that.

Ironically, where science could really provide a return on investment, it is not applied. There is a tremendous need to use the latest scientific advances in predictive technologies at the point where development candidates are chosen to enter a development programme. Much can be achieved these days in predicting issues, using computer simulation and testing in animal and human tissue, for example (in silico and ex vivo techniques). Sadly, the prospect of getting into clinical trials attracts far more attention, as the valley of death is about to claim another victim.

This is why I am arguing that Big Pharma needs a lesson in science.

ENDS

Systems thinking expert Peter Checkland makes this point nicely with his soft systems methodology. Science is a vitally important discipline in which, as Checkland[xviii] puts it, "the highest value attaches to the advancement of knowledge." Scientists are trained to use reductionist thinking: running experiments and drawing conclusions from them. Checkland compares this way of working with the mind-set of engineers and technologists, who "prize most highly the efficient accomplishment of some defined purpose."

He provides an example of his work in the science-based Imperial Chemical Industries. His team was charged with developing synthetic leather to seize a market opportunity. A research scientist gave the project a negative response. Checkland reports his comment: "The three dimensional matrix of natural leather is so complex that it cannot at present be accurately described; therefore we cannot hope to simulate it."

The research scientist assumed that the question was about furthering scientific knowledge. Checkland's observation was: "Had [the scientist] assumed the question to be a technological one, he would have asked not 'can we copy leather?' but 'can we imagine a material which will perform satisfactorily in end users' hands in which natural leather is now used?'" The search is then totally different. It is about finding an alternative solution to an end user's problem.

This is a vitally important distinction when developing products. How many companies are studying their molecules and materials rather than developing solutions for patients? We know from the US GAO figures that on average, they are studying 10,000 molecules for every one that gets to market.

Here then, we argue that Big Pharma companies are selecting compounds (development candidates) to register for sale when they have no idea about their chances of success. We are not saying they should be certain, because nothing in life is, but they should make a sufficient attempt to thoroughly check the robustness of the candidate for the rigors ahead, the journey through the valley of death.

---

xviii. Checkland, Peter, Systems *Thinking, Systems Practice*, J Wiley & Sons, 1999

73

Daniel Steenstra, the Royal Academy of Engineering's visiting professor of medical innovation at Cranfield University, reinforces this message.

Steenstra is a qualified medic working in the field of engineering. I had contacted him via LinkedIn to ask whether he would be interested in working with me on a funding bid in advanced manufacturing supply chain in life science for Oxford BioMedica. He called me a few weeks later.

The bid was successful and raised £7.1 million ($11 million) from the UK government to work in the important field of gene therapy manufacturing. Steenstra's views on science and innovation are spot-on from my perspective. Here is what he has to say on the matter:

AN EXPERT WITNESS STATEMENT: PROFESSOR DANIEL STEENSTRA

Q. How would you sum up the Pharma approach to product development?

A. Pharma might spend lots of money on R&D, but the evidence suggests that it is simply not effective. Take the astronomical attrition rates, or the years it takes from the discovery of the new compound to market launch. New pharmaceuticals such as monoclonal antibodies or genetic therapies take decades. Other sectors are far more driven by the end users and have developed a set of processes to meet their customers' needs, such as concurrent engineering, rapid prototyping, lean manufacturing that are yet to be used in the Pharma sector. It's time that the Pharma companies stop doing the wrong things. Take their heads out of the sand and look around at how other companies do it.

Q. Can you tell us something about the attitude to innovation you have experienced?

A. Many companies and individuals are still confused about innovation and still think it's about creativity, coming up with new ideas. That's only the beginning. Innovation is the successful commercialization of a new idea. That means it's the blood, sweat, and tears that turn ideas into benefits:

making money from it or delivering better and higher-quality health care. Innovation needs new ideas. It needs research and development to create and develop these ideas further into new products or services.

Q. So what are scientific ideas to innovation then?

A. To use the old chicken-and-egg metaphor—the seeds (as in chicken feed) are the creative ideas; the egg is the successful outcome—the innovation. The chicken is the organization that with its R&D, sales and marketing, manufacturing and supply chain processes turns the "feed" into "eggs." Furthermore, there are different types of innovation:

- incremental innovation, the small changes and updates that make a product a little faster, lighter, cheaper, or of better quality
- radical innovation, based on a technology that has never been used, such as the first CT scan combing X-ray with computer technology
- disruptive innovation, based on a simplifying technology that requires less skill and can be applied in a more convenient environment, such as a drug eluting stent rather than coronary bypass surgery

In reality, the Pharmaceutical sector is more complex that the chicken and the egg.

In my experience, R&D in the Pharma sector is very much uppercase 'R' and very lowercase 'd.' It is too focused on the compound or the new Pharmaceutical technology itself and ignores who is going to use it, where and how it will be applied, and who will pay for it. It has too much technology push rather than consumer (patient or health care professional) pull.

ENDS

So the point Steenstra makes is that scientific invention—a good idea—is not an innovation until it becomes a product in the end user's hands. Now we turn to the beast that is snapping up all the inventions and ideas.

The valley of death is stealing our drugs

The Charge of the Light Brigade

Half a league, half a league,
Half a league onward,
All in the valley of Death
Rode the six hundred.
"Forward, the Light Brigade!
Charge for the guns!" he said:
Into the valley of Death
Rode the six hundred.

"Forward, the Light Brigade!"
Was there a man dismay'd ?
Not tho' the soldier knew
Someone had blunder'd:
Their's not to make reply,
Their's not to reason why,
Their's but to do and die:
Into the valley of Death
Rode the six hundred....

In his famous poem, Alfred Lord Tennyson describes soldiers embarking on a suicide mission, totally unaware of the wall of fire they were to face, "'Charge for the guns!' he said"; their superiors ordered the charge. "Not tho' the soldier knew Someone had blunder'd." Someone had certainly blundered, and in Big Pharma the same blunder continues to be repeated. Compounds are entering the development pipeline completely unprepared for the rigors ahead, and the canons have become bigger and louder over the years as regulators demand ever-greater standards from the industry and governments look for value for money from their health-care budgets. What is driving this then?

The patent clock is running the show

The motivation for the charge Lord Tennyson described was the dreadful imperative of war. What is it now for Big Pharma? It is the crack of the starting pistol once the patent clock has been set.

Somewhere during the Find It stage, the company registers the molecule with the patent office. This sets a definite date for expiration of the patent-protection umbrella. The patent clock is now ticking. Every day spent on selecting a development candidate to head for the valley, and every day spent on File It, is a day lost to sales in the market in the minds of all involved—assuming, of course, that it gets to market. Given the statistic in Figure 13 above, there is only a one in 250 chance of the molecule getting to market, so there is little appetite for spending time or money on its future. Everyone waits to see what the clinical data will look like some five to ten years later.

The harsh reality here is of more haste and less of speed. In the frantic effort to get into the clinic as quickly as possible, Pharma does not take the time to select its runners carefully. The more runners there are, the thinking goes, the greater the likelihood that one of them will get through the process.

As the valley becomes deeper and wider, Big Pharma has become increasingly less-equipped to make the journey because of the emaciated state of its FILE IT capability, which is now predominantly in the hands of third parties or strangers, as we go on to explore.

Strangers are sailing the ship

To do justice to this next reality, I start with an expert witness, Professor Andrew Cox. The professor is world renowned in strategic procurement and outsourcing practices and in my estimation is the only academic who truly understands the nature of the business of procuring goods and services from third parties. He is in great demand across all industrial sectors and has kindly offered his views here on practices in the Pharma industry.

AN EXPERT WITNESS STATEMENT:
Professor Andrew Cox

Q. Is Big Pharma alone in adopting less-than-optimal practices in outsourcing?

A. Many industries have extensive experience of less-than-optimal make versus buy decision-making and outsourcing, and the major pharmaceutical companies are no different in this respect. Most poor practice arises from low levels of professional competence and a lack of rigorous and robust make versus buy and outsourcing management methodologies. Readers wishing to dig deeper can find more at *Strategic Outsourcing & Critical Asset Management*, IIAPS White Paper 15/3, www.iiaps.org,[xix] and *Andrew Cox, Sourcing Portfolio Analysis, 2014*[xx]).

Q. What is your perspective on Pharma specifically?

A. In the last few decades, the major pharmaceutical companies appear to have been influenced by a number of factors when outsourcing many of their former key internal resources and capabilities (critical assets) to the suppliers in its supply chains. The key factors appear to have been:

- a desire for more flexible use of assets
- lower perceived costs of external (developing country) supply
- short-term headcount cost reduction targets to meet quarterly financial targets
- copying the latest fad.

Q. I can see your first bullet could be for strategic reasons, but the other three appear to be based on ill-informed decision making. Is that right?

A. I'm glad you raised the point and of course you are right. The remaining three bullets reflect incompetence in the make-versus-buy decision,

---

xix. http://www.iiaps.org/

xx. http://www.amazon.co.uk/Sourcing-Portfolio-Analysis-Positioning-Management/dp/1873439547 and knock-on management issues that can occur once the contract is signed, normally caused by three major factors:

- Unforeseen loss of critical assets. By this, I mean inadvertent outsourcing of assets that provide the basis for differentiating your product from the competition.
- Unforeseen postcontractual moral hazard. This may sound a difficult concept, but in fact it is easily explained. It means that once the contract is signed, there is a shift in the power and leverage position of the buyer and supplier over time. I sometimes lightheartedly use the analogy of my marriage contract with Mrs. Cox and how our power and leverage positions have changed over time.
- Inability to drive improvement in the supply and value chain. This last point relates to the relative weakening of a buyer's position so that it cannot drive through the necessary improvement work that is going to make them more competitive in the market. More powerful suppliers will not be obliged to offer up improved quality, reduced costs or end-user value enhancements in the end-to-end value stream unless there is a consequent return for them. If the contract assures their return anyway, then more often than not it does not make business sense for suppliers to offer things up.

Q. What evidence have you to offer up from your professional expertise in this area?

A. Unfortunately for the major pharmaceutical companies that used to be the "channel captains" who controlled the industry and all of its major supply chains through a judicious control internally of critical assets, there has been considerable evidence of very poor practice in outsourcing in recent years. This has led to the loss of critical assets, postcontractual moral hazard and poor postcontractual management of suppliers. Evidence of this poor practice is listed below:

Unforeseen loss of critical assets: There has been a loss of internal intellectual property (IP) and technical design, manufacturing and quality-control competencies, with growing dependency on suppliers for these key competencies.

Unforeseen postcontractual moral hazards:

- There has been an Increase in regulatory and supply-chain complexity, with increased threats to corporate reputation and litigation.
- There has been an increasing and unanticipated dependency on supply-chain partnerships with distributors and manufacturers.
- There has been a failure to predict the size of switching costs and high exit barriers for Big Pharma companies with their key suppliers.

Inability to drive value for money improvement in the supply and value chain:

- There has been increasing evidence of poor quality control and adulteration of raw materials, products, and services across the industry.
- There is widespread evidence of poor schedule compliance and on-time delivery.
- The major Pharmaceutical companies have been experiencing rising rather than falling prices and total costs of ownership.
- There is considerable evidence that the major pharmaceutical companies still lack cross-functional supply-chain value and process optimization competence.

Q. How would you sum up all of this?

A. All of these recent developments lead to a serious questioning of the strategic outsourcing undertaken by the major pharmaceutical companies in the recent past. Not only has there been an inadvertent loss of critical assets, but also an increase in competition and a loss of control of key suppliers and supply chains. Unfortunately, this has occurred at a time when competition from generic companies has increased and when profits from patented products have been in decline. The result has been an industry experiencing widespread decline in profitability, now responding with short-term knee-jerk merger and acquisition strategies. This is a telling indictment of the failure of strategic outsourcing in the pharmaceutical industry.

ENDS

These are powerful words and should send a chill through the hearts of industry executives. "This is a telling indictment of the failure of strategic outsourcing in the Pharmaceutical industry," the professor concludes.

There is so much for readers to pick up on here, and I hope the issues shine through. The key harsh reality I want to follow up is Professor Cox's comment "Major pharmaceutical companies that used to be the 'channel captains.'"

This is why this section is titled *Strangers are Sailing the Ship*. We can confidently say that no other industry has outsourced its critical assets to the extent Big Pharma has. It has now lost the ability to design and develop its products because suppliers and contractors hold the key, and it has become a golden key for them.

Boeing dabbled with increased levels of outsourced development for the Dreamliner and suffered a reported eighteen-month delay, as well as much pain and suffering, for its troubles. This is what Peter S. Cohan reported in his book *You Can't Order Change: Lessons from Jim McNerney's Turnaround at Boeing* (Hardcover—December 26, 2008).[xxi] "But by outsourcing both the design and the manufacturing, Boeing lost control of the development process." The point McNerney makes is that outsourcing manufacture can work so long as the development process and control are in the hands of the developer and it allows detailed instructions and specifications to be handed down to contractors and suppliers. This

---

xxi. http://www.dailyfinance.com/2011/01/21/boeing-dreamliner-delays-outsourcing-goes-too-far/

has not been the case for a long time in Pharma. The knowledge, experience, and capabilities all lie within the supply base.

Observations, Views, and Experiences of the Author

If I were to appear on British television's *Mastermind* quiz show, this would be my specialty subject. I've been involved in procuring almost every good and service Pharma could ever want, from molecular modeling software to third-party finished goods channel distribution services across global markets and everything in between. Through the years, I have seen the Pharma purchasers get ever more locked into their contractor supply bases, and this is why. When the industry decided to mass outsource, it did not take account of the regulatory environment in which it operated. This environment prevents any company from using a contractor unless that contractor has been registered as part of the regulatory filing. The result is that any company in the filing, especially if it is the only one, is in a powerful position because the switching costs and regulatory turmoil would be enormous.

Now in the power position, contractors often are able to name their prices and charge for every little piece of work. I was at a large contract manufacturer where one of the senior executives recounted how a client complained about having to pay for the number of investigations and corrective actions. The client was charged for putting things right when they went wrong at the contractor's premises.

ENDS

Even if Big Pharma remained the channel captain, there would be a further intractable obstacle in the way of taking hold of the effort to develop medicine for patients—the massive gulf between Big Pharma and the end users of its products, health-care professionals.

There is a massive gulf between health-care professionals and Big Pharma

This harsh reality is about the distance between companies developing drugs and the end users. The most contact drug developers have with health-care providers is between the developing company's clinical group (often a contract research organization) and the clinical trial study investigators who operate within a network of hospitals and clinics signed up for the trials. The communication is pretty much one way; the investigator role is to collect data from recruits on the clinical trial. The developer has to give a brochure telling the investigator everything about the product undergoing the testing. The objective is to collect the clinical data until the end of the study, normally blind to both the investigator and patient for phase II studies and beyond.

On completion of the study, the statistical end point gets either a pass or fail. Each phase of development has a new end point:

- preclinical proof of safety
- clinical proof of safety (phase I)
- further clinical proof of safety and efficacy (phases II and III).

Drugs reaching their end points are met with fanfares and the waving of flags. Press announcements follow, and plans are put into place for the journey to the next end point. Similar celebrations take place if that also succeeds, until that one in 250 reaches the approval of a drug for patients.

During this time, the drug developer fixes its eyes firmly on the regulator, with the case report form representing the patient. The case report form records everything that has happened to the patient during the trial for inclusion in the regulatory filing dossier. It can be electronic or paper.

The net result is that patients and the many health-care professionals are not on the radar screen during the development stage as the Pharma companies and regulatory authorities do their dance. Let's discuss regulatory authorities when it comes to this gap.

Regulators are getting in the way of the patient-provider interface

For this point, I need to bring in reinforcements because this is not an area of my work. The expert witness is Dr. Gary Acton. We have

83

worked together on three occasions, at Vanguard Medica circa 2000, Neuropharm circa 2007, and Antisoma circa 2009. As is the silo nature of this industry, we interacted only through the odd nod in the corridor and quick niceties as we changed companies. In work terms, clinical directors and commercial supply chain folk were a million miles apart—intentionally.

Dr. Acton and I have kept in touch over the years, and I was delighted to read his book on life in oncology development, *Sympathy for the Devil*. It is beautifully written. We will hear from Dr. Acton again later, but first we need to hear his thoughts on regulation and the clinic. I offer a word of warning: Dr. Acton does not mince words.

Q. What do you think of the current patient-provider interface?

A. That is best answered with a recent example of the difficulties and dilemmas we all face, when having to deal with recalcitrant regulation presented by the extraordinary trans-Atlantic story of the use of Avastin in breast cancer, which has resulted in greater US-European acrimony than at any other time since the American War of Independence of three centuries ago.

Avastin (bevacizumab) is a novel antibody treatment that targets the profuse blood supply upon which tumors depend for their survival, rather than attacking the cancer cells themselves. When combined with conventional chemotherapy, it should therefore provide a double-barreled shotgun blast to predatory malignancies. The drug has proved hugely successful, with a firmly established role in the management of bowel, kidney, brain, lung, ovarian, and cervical cancers, conditions in which it has made a meaningful improvement in the lives of those suffering from these dreadful diseases.

Overall, it is a revolutionary drug. No other biotechnology product has such a wide range of uses. Although it doesn't actually cure anyone of their cancer, it clearly arrests the spread of the disease and buys patients valuable time, something they would otherwise fast be running out of.

However, it is strangely absent, at least in the United States, as a treatment option for breast cancer, one of the most common and devastating of all malignant diagnoses.

Avastin was made available for use in metastatic breast cancer in Europe way back in 2007. The drug continues to be used with benefit in hundreds of thousands of women every year throughout the European community. The approval was on the basis of a single study (called the E2100 trial) which showed that Avastin, combined with the chemotherapy drug paclitaxel, markedly slowed the rate at which the disease progressed. There wasn't really any controversy over it. Certainly nothing like the anguished torment of the debate that was eventually to rage in the United States over whether the drug should be allowed to reach and remain on the market.

The European Medicines Agency has repeatedly reaffirmed its allegiance to the results of E2100, despite the complexities introduced by subsequent North American developments. In December 2010, the agency's advisory committee, Committee on Human Medicinal Products, concluded that "Avastin (with paclitaxel) has been convincingly shown to prolong progression-free survival, without a negative effect on overall survival."

In the opinion of the European Medicines Agency itself, in February 2011, "the results of existing studies on the combination of bevacizumab and paclitaxel are consistent and support a positive effect of therapy with a clear benefit to patients."

It couldn't be any clearer than that—at least by the opaque standards of a regulator.

In the middle of 2011, the European Medicines Agency had even gone that extra mile and approved Avastin in combination with another chemotherapy drug called capecitabine, showing that it was prepared to stand its ground and make a drug that clearly worked as widely available to as many women as possible.

In America, however, the situation could not have been more different. In 2011, Avastin's fate in breast cancer was on the line in the United States despite a total of three Phase III trials supporting its value in this disease. The drug was widely used in at least eighty-four countries around the world. But in the United States, it was suddenly fighting for its very existence. Its enemy was none other than the regulators themselves. Patients and clinicians alike looked on in horror as the conflict unfolded. There was a very real possibility that they were about to be deprived of the world's best-selling cancer drug.

Having a drug reach the market is the single dream shared by everyone in biotechnology. Just the possibility of it is enough to counteract the innumerable nightmares caused by all the other drugs that fall by the wayside. But the biggest nightmare of all is the possibility of losing a drug once it has made it through the approval process. The prospect of having a drug withdrawn after it has become comfortably ensconced in the marketplace would cause even the most battle-hardened biotechnology veteran to buckle at the knees.

Once a drug has survived the arduous journey through the development jungle, it ought to be safe and secure when it emerges on the other side. If it hasn't perished along the way, it should be allowed to prosper. But nothing is forever in cancer medicine. Now and then, drugs end up being ejected from the market despite their best attempts. New data can emerge about the safety or efficacy, which puts the drugs in a worse light and forces a reappraisal of their viability. It's like having parole revoked and being sent back to prison.

On the rare occasions when this happens, it's the biotechnology equivalent of a natural disaster. Moreover, when it affects the world's biggest biotechnology company and involves its best-selling and most successful cancer drug, it's an earthquake measuring a ten on the Richter scale. The reverberations and aftershocks are felt everywhere. No one and nothing is safe. The ensuing tsunami sweeps away all in front of it.

In the summer of 2010, biotechnology was facing its worst-ever humanitarian crisis. There was a very real prospect that Genentech's Avastin, one of the most widely used cancer drugs in existence, might lose its position in the marketplace in the United States. The unthinkable looked like it might become the unavoidable.

It is difficult to accurately convey the scope of this development. If Avastin, the granddaddy of them all, wasn't safe, then absolutely nothing else was either. It represented a threat to the very viability of drug development in cancer. Having reached the face of the gold seam, the mine was in danger of being blown up. Who would want to carry on prospecting when confronted with hazards like that? It was like spending all your life paying off the mortgage and then having the bank repossess your home anyway. In this case, though, the house is worth several billion dollars.

ENDS

If we are to believe Dr. Acton, there are concerning issues with the regulatory interface between those developing drugs and the health-care professionals involved. This relates not only to the regulatory arena.

If the regulators say, "Jump," the industry says, "How High?"

This is commonly accepted throughout the industry. The regulators are omnipotent. What they say goes. The industry has stopped thinking for itself as it hangs on to regulators' apron strings. To confirm this is Peter Savin, former VP, Global Quality Assurance at GlaxoSmithKline, now editor of the journal GMP Review, and an industry consultant like myself.

AN EXPERT WITNESS STATEMENT: PETER SAVIN

Q. What is your view on the industry's lead from the regulators?

A. First, many thanks for the opportunity to contribute to your quest and to comment on one of my biggest concerns for the future of our industry, namely the ever-increasing levels of mandate and documentation that we face in our daily operations.

I need to say that the Industry must grow up. It needs to move away from the child-parent relationship it has allowed to develop with the regulators. Waiting to be told what to do, by regulators and the ensuing consultants, isn't a good sign of organizational capability or a mature culture. If you doubt the depth of this child-parent dependence, when you next attend a conference with presentations from both regulatory and industry speakers, just take time to notice how the room fills up when the regulatory speakers are on stage and how everyone is listening intently and studiously taking pages of notes. Then compare this to the attendance and attention when the industry speakers are on stage.

Q. I've witnessed that for myself many times. What impact do you think this dependence has had on working practices in the industry?

A. Having worked for forty years in the industry, mostly in manufacturing quality and latterly as a consultant, I've had the opportunity to see the birth of good manufacturing practice and how it has grown and matured. Correspondingly, I've also seen that the biggest and ever-increasing risk that pharmaceutical manufacturing operations face is that of regulatory noncompliance. It saddens me that the public and regulatory perception of our industry and the trust they have in us has plummeted in the past ten years, from being the most ethical industry to being ranked alongside the oil and banking industries. This decline has been caused largely by increasing regulatory censure and the sheer size of fines being imposed on companies through the US legal system. Something needs to be done to reverse this downward trend in our reputation, and we need to address the compliance issue as a first step.

Q. What do you think is at the bottom of this trend?

A. The behavior of the industry, as it aspires to continually demonstrate compliance in the dynamic and growing regulatory environment, means that already well-controlled companies often try to show they are better than the regulations and implement more procedures, controls, and monitoring than are necessary. In addition, the typical response from companies facing regulatory censure is an explosion of self-imposed policies, procedures, and documentation, often advised by some pharmaceutical consultants that strive to prove their value.

We fail to understand that the consequence of what we are doing is actually worse than zero payback. The almost exponential increase in documentation has ironically been accompanied by a significant increase in regulatory criticism of companies. There is a clear link between procedural noncompliances and complaints with the increase in documentation.

For some reason, there is a commonly held belief that the best response to regulatory censure is to generate more paperwork. It is sad, but true, that GMP really has come to mean great mountains of paperwork rather than good manufacturing practice. What is also true is that this has not resulted in better-quality products, although in the United States it has enabled huge fines to be extracted from Pharma companies. But that is another topic worthy of open discussion.

So the root causes of the problems lie with both the regulators and the industry itself. Both fail to recognize that this continual drive for ever-increasing complexity is not sustainable, and it certainly isn't intelligent. Remember the saying, "Any intelligent fool can make things bigger and more complex. It takes a touch of genius and a lot of courage to move in the opposite direction." It is time for the foolishness of unnecessary complexity to stop and courage to be demonstrated throughout the industry.

ENDS

There is serious work to be done then to rectify this debilitating relationship problem.

Now we move on to the effects of advanced therapies and diagnostics on the industry.

Patient markets are shrinking irreversibly

The size of markets for Pharma products is shrinking with the realization that many drugs help only a certain proportion of those on clinical trials, not the entire population for the disease state. With the emergence of genetic testing and more powerful diagnosis, we are likely to find approved drugs applying to much smaller patient groups, thus reducing the sales revenue, unless the industry increases prices.

What we have learned of stratified and personalized medicine is going to make this even more extreme and force companies to think more carefully and deeply about the patients they serve. The question arises as to whether Pharma companies will be able to operate over so many diverse disease areas. The emergence of stratified medicine is set to demand ever-deepening knowledge banks of people's biological characteristics with respect to particular diseased states. The critical mass required to build these knowledge bases is likely to severely restrict coverage across multiple therapeutic areas.

Pharma marketing has lost its way

Pharma spends significant time, effort and mountains of cash on marketing their product portfolios. Is that really money and effort well directed?

To help us with this topic, we turn to our expert witness, Dr Graham Cox, Principal Consultant at KASOCIO. After a few chat's on skype, I realised Graham was not the typical Pharma senior marketing executive. He was firmly rooted in the reality of what is going wrong and active in plotting a path for the future.

This is what he has to say on the subject:

Q. What's the problem with marketing in Pharma?

A. Before I answer that lets get back to basics. Making products that do things, telling people about them and selling them is a process that has been going on for many thousands of years. However, it might have been the great industrial revolution that led to a more formal recognition of what we might call Marketing 1.0 which was 'tell people about your product and some buy it'. Maybe this was the age of advertising where the bigger the spend and the more creative the advert, the more the company sold. A huge over simplification but I hope you'll agree, things were a bit more straightforward then.

Then in the 1970's and 80's the market research 'industry' gained momentum to give rise to Marketing 2.0. This new marketing model was based on the seemingly obvious truth that 'if you find out what people want, then go and make it, there will be a market ready and waiting for your product/service'. The sophistication (or should I say complexity) of the market research machine in driving decision-making has become so engrained into our thinking that for many, it would be foolish to make anything (a concept, a product etc.) without involving in depth market research at every step of the way. Most non-Pharma companies have moved on to Marketing 3.0 but Pharma still supports departments and an industry that churns out data that has never been proven to help in decision-making.

Q. Why do you think Pharma has been left behind?

A. Pharma is a very conservative business and getting change takes a long time. Here's an example; Using Marketing 2.0 thinking, Pharma regularly spends huge sums of money on 'conjoint' analyses (from $650K to well over $1M). This is a piece of market research that claims to measure customer preference structures. Companies feed in potential promotional 'claims' for the drug and using clever software algorithms the conjoint 'black box' spews out preference share for combinations of 'claims'. It sounds too good to be true and indeed it is. Although its easy to see how any company would like to know how much sales they can attach to a set of claims, pretty much all of this has been proven to be no more accurate as much smaller and zero cost internal conjoints (Satter and Hensel-Börner, In Conjoint Measurement: Methods and Applications: 2000, Springer Verlag, Berlin, p121-133). In addition psychological tests have shown quite clearly that what people say they might do (preference share) has little bearing on what they actually do (market share and sales). As other industries move on, Pharma is left with historic templated budgets that need to be spent (or it will be lost next year and look 'odd' against other drug budgets in the pipeline). So rather than review the value of these expensive exercises they continue to hide behind them blindly making decisions on flawed methodology.

Q. So are Pharma wasting money on un proven market research?

A. Indeed. Marketing continues to have huge un-questioned budgets to hold 'Think Tanks', panel discussions and the obligatory advisory boards. Although asking customers what they want all sounds logical most of this is a total waste of money. Experiments conducted using functional MRI (fMRI) clearly demonstrate fundamental flaws in our thinking about what traditional market research can tell us and what it can't. Yet Pharma seem trapped holding a perception where they feel 'naked' without having this (largely consensus driven) information to convince the company the drug is on the right track. The market research industry feeds off this lack of confidence and promises better decision making but delivers 'accurately wrong' rather than 'roughly right' results. With only 1 in 4 launched drugs ever repaying it's R&D cost, the logic and justification for this huge market research spend just doesn't hold.

Q. So it's really just 'bad science'?

A. Ironic isn't it, but yes. I would say though that great marketing is a blend of pressure testing prototype ideas and taking bold decisions. Many have read about huge marketing blunders where the logic seems straight forward but the product didn't sell. A lot of the reasons for failure is in the methodology of the market research. If you take advertising slogans or messages, these are traditionally tested with customers sometimes across many countries. The intention is to get a set of messages that resonate with the customer. However, many market research agencies tend to aggregate responses so the client gets to choose the messages that 'on average' the sample customers liked. Unfortunately creating a successful product isn't like that. Polarising customer views is what creates success. Take Rolex, Porche, Apple etc. Although highly successful, its easy to find people that really dislike what they stand for... and that's the crux of it. A Pharma brand needs to stand for something, but most products end up right in the graveyard of 'average' because they avoid clear polarising messages and instead plump for the 'safe' middle ground. The conservative scientific thinking of Pharma always like to be in the safe zone although its far from safe when looking at the resultant sales.

ENDS

Much food for thought here, and more to follow.

New business models are sitting on a knife edge

This next reality is based on Big Pharma being the alpha male of the industry. Biotech and Virtual Pharma need to make deals with the large Pharma companies to survive. Companies in generics and biosimilars depend on Big Pharma to get the original patented products onto the market. The huge contractor base would fall apart if they could not build their business plans on work coming from the Big Pharma world; and wholesalers would have no products to buy and sell without Big Pharma loading the pipeline.

If we continue on the current trajectory, there is every chance that the industry will fall like a house of cards.

Governments pouring money into science won't help

For all the scientific grant funding and various other supporting financial initiatives on Governmental menus globally, it will be to no avail unless the issues we discuss above are addressed at a fundamental level. More of the same will not cut the mustard.

Here in the UK we are bombarded almost daily with multi-million pound funding calls to solve this or that particular scientific conundrum; similarly for the European landscape, and no doubt it is the same in most other countries across the globe, as they to seek to capitalize on future opportunities in 21st century healthcare.

Hopefully, readers will have gleaned that availability of funds is much less of an issue than finding the individuals and companies that are able to translate science into workable solutions for patients and health-care professionals, often with extremely modest budgets.

Universities and colleges have caught the science bug

Using no science whatsoever, I did a webseach on *university courses in pharmaceuticals and biopharmaceuticals.* Below is the resulting summary I was able to piece together by randomly selecting from the content of courses on offer. Hopefully the following is indicative of the issue we face.

BSc in Pharmaceuticals/Pharmaceutics
First year

- Compounding
- Formulation Chemistry
- Pharmaceutical Processes and Technologies
- Basic Microbiology
- Professional and Quantitative Science Skills
- Cell Biology and Biochemistry

Second year

- Product Formulation
- Chemical Analysis, Quality and Stability
- Applied Pharmacology
- Pharmaceutical Microbiology
- Product Formulation

Third year

- Quality Assurance and Quality by Design Principles
- Project
- Development and Manufacture of Pharmaceutical Products
- Pharmaceutical Materials Science

MSc in Pharmaceuticals/Biopharmaceuticals

- Dosage Forms and Pharmacokinetics
- Delivering Gene and Therapeutic Proteins
- Essential Research and Study Skills
- Research Manipulation
- Pharmaceutical Nanotechnology
- Gene Cloning, Expression and Analysis
- Bioinformatics
- Entrepreneurship and Innovation
- Research Project

These are of course essential skills for those embarking and moving onward with careers in the pharmaceutical and biopharmaceutical industry. Note however, the absence of translational skills to accompany these skills and also the lack of focus on end products. The only mention of manufacture in the BSc programme is in the third year of study; and for the MSc, it doesn't even make the starting grid.

The harsh reality is that universities and colleges are setting and reinforcing a reductionist-thinking mentality that stays with its offspring for life.

CHAPTER 8

THE FOG OF CONFUSION IS LIFTED

Armed with newfound confidence of knowing what the harsh realities really are, we can now turn back to our questions amid the fog. We ask each question again and answer them in five words or less. This is so the dissenting voices from chapter 5 are clear on the message and have an opportunity to critique.

It's not easy to separate vested interests from genuine confusion over what has happened. Fortunately, it is not necessary to make that distinction because the facts are now laid bare before them and the opportunity exists to confirm or deny accordingly.

Is drug development really a risky business?
Yes, but it shouldn't be.

Does it cost a fortune to develop a new drug?
Yes, but It shouldn't.

Are some drugs too expensive?
Yes.

Is Big Pharma becoming more focused on the patient these days?
No.

Is there a lack of innovation in drug development?
Yes.

Is there too much sales in Pharma?
Yes.

Do drug side effects get proper attention?
No.

Are copycat drugs (generics) the same as the original?
No.

Is it necessary to continue testing in animals?
It shouldn't be.

Is the Big Pharma supply chain in trouble?
Yes.

These are the straight answers to some crucial questions, but others remain.

For example, it is reported that quality levels are poor in Pharma manufacturing, typically well below those of the semiconductor, automotive, and aerospace industries. As a rule of thumb, Pharma produces 70,000 to 100,000 defects for every one million items produced. For the other industries, it is closer to 3.4 defects per one million produced units.

G. K. Raju confirmed the figures in an article titled "Pharmaceutical manufacturing – what needs to change?" in 2012[xxii], "The industry overall still operates at the same sigma level of 2.5 to 3 that it did last decade," Raju said.

For those not familiar with the terminology, sigma level refers to the number of defects within a total population of events if they were normally distributed. Exemplary industries achieve six sigma levels, which is 3.4 defects per million. 2.5 to 3.0 sigma in Pharma relates to throwing away 7 percent to 10 percent of what is produced.

That is quite a difference and should be explained. Leaning on the harsh realities we have outlined above, we can forward some thoughts.

---

xxii. http://www.rmg-uk.com/pharmaceutical-manufacturing-what-needs-to-change/

By ushering potentially active molecules into safety testing on the basis of an unproven scientific theory and testing of a few grams in a test tube, we sidestep principles of proper quality in manufacturing. These principles are based on designing quality into your product, building meaningful, long-term relationships with suppliers, and streamlining the end-to-end flow of materials.

In Pharma, the underpinning supplier relationships are based on scientific exchanges between the two sides and a purchase order to seal the deal. Often, each group of scientists selects its own preferred suppliers, normally based on criteria related to science, interesting technology, or a shared sporting interest. Rarely, if ever, is supplier selection based on long-term needs of the market.

Soon, we have a multitude of suppliers and contractors, each with a finger in the pie, as the outsourcing boom has continued. By the time we get into phase III manufacture, the end-to-end supply chain is a spaghetti-like construction spanning the globe. Now, any kind of quality enhancement is all but lost.

We pick it up back at the Morgans' farmhouse table, as they contemplate where their cosy life style selling succulent sausages has left them. Dafydd has managed to get the right person to the farm to discuss the issues.

A Helpful Metaphor

Rhys Rees, a local businessman from the next valley over, was sitting at the table in front of the family. The family explained all that had transpired. Rhys listened intently and then said, "So, if I got this right, you managed to start selling succulent sausages to a far-off country a long time ago, and that worked well for a period." The family nodded enthusiastically. "Then you sold off a bunch of the machines that had been making the sausages, the people who worked them, and the people who were developing those sausages for you. Yes?"

"I suppose so," Morgan said as the enthusiasm began to wane.

"You also stopped making those sausages when the queen stopped giving you preferential pricing?"

"Yes, we did," Morgan said weakly.

"What pricing was the queen suggesting for those sausages?"

The family members looked at one another. Dafydd took over from his father. "I'm not sure we ever thought to ask."

Rhys tried not to look surprised. "What's done is done," he said. "We have to deal with the now, starting with a review of where this strategy has left you—but that's for next time we meet."

"One last question," Rhys said. "Have you ever heard of a Triple-F strategy?"

"Not really" said Dafydd. "Should we have?"

"No, of course not. It was just a random thought."

ENDS

Rhys summed up the problem pretty well, don't you think?

We now leave the world of Pharma present to contemplate the future.

PART III PHARMA FUTURE

CHAPTER 9

Exploring Rehabilitation For The Industry

"Insanity: doing the same thing over and over
again and expecting different results."
—Albert Einstein

This is a much-used quote from the professor, but it is the quintessential definition of insanity. In the face of all that has transpired, Big Pharma still appears to be beating its head against the wall and wondering about the source of the headache. How long can Pharma hold it all together as the forces of nature close in?

Big Pharma defies gravity

Yes, Big Pharma companies have managed to defy the laws of gravity, with crucial flaws for a long time. Eventually, though, they must come back down to earth. No business has ever survived in the long term without consistently engaging with the end users of its products, predicting their needs, and delivering value for the money propositions it has developed with end users in mind. Big Pharma has survived by going in the opposite direction: developing products and then looking for end users in need of what they have, and using sales and marketing to lead the charge. As we learned earlier, this was the case in many sectors fifty or more years ago; then the world moved on. The panic and confusion we saw in chapter 6 are manifestations of the forces dragging these companies back to earth. The universe is trying to pass on an important message.

As we prepare to dive into the specifics of rehabilitation, we must accept this as the stark reality. In the same way that acceptance of an addiction is the first stage on the road to recovery, so Big Pharma must make that painful acknowledgment, to open the floodgates to change.

Now might be an opportune moment to return to the Morgan family and listen to what consultant Rhys Rees has to say about the predicament:

A Helpful Metaphor

Rhys Rees looked Morgan Morgan straight in the eye from across the table. "You've been living in Cloud Cuckooland all these years, my friend. Sorry to be so direct, but you have to know the truth."

"Don't worry, Rhys, you're only confirming what we already know—now. We've been fools," Morgan said with a side glance toward Morfydd, who had never before heard him concede defeat.

"Well, I said I could help you last time I came, said Rhys, and that's what I'm going to do. Only you have to drop all these silly ideas about making a quick buck selling succulent sausages to strangers, and you have to go right back to where you started: aiming to help protein-deficient patients living on a vegetarian diet."

"How much do you know about the wise men who diagnosed the need for protein in these subjects' diet?" Rhys asked.

"Not a lot," said Morgan, looking at Dafydd for help.

"Dad's right, Rhys, said Dafydd. We had some contact with a few of them in the early days, but once we got the approval to sell, we left it to the salespeople to visit them. They never said a word other than report their sales figures. We weren't going to ask any questions, just in case the bubble burst."

Rhys probed further. "So where did you think the money was going to come from once those succulent sausages lost their sizzle?"

Dafydd replied, "We always thought if we could do it once, we just had to keep on with the formula and eventually we'd be set up again. That was before we realized most of our sausage meat was going into the bin, even the sausages that we thought were home and dry. It wasn't long before you came on to the scene, Rhys, that we realized the formula wasn't working."

Rhys leaned toward Dafydd to add gravity to his next question. "What made you believe you could repeat the formula at the same time as ditching all those sausage machines and the people working them?"

"I know, I know, groaned Dafydd, hindsight is a wonderful thing, but as I said, it's only just dawned on us that developing succulent sausages is not as easy as it seemed, especially when you are asking employees that you sacked to do all the legwork."

The final question from Rhys turned back to Morgan Morgan. "If you had to do it over again, Morgan, what would you have the family do differently?"

Morgan thought for a second or two and then said, "I'd have us spend quality time with the wise men and the suffering subjects, finding out about their conditions and developing sausages only where we thought there was a good chance of success. We'd have to make small prototype sausages in their skins and test them thoroughly to make sure they have the right level of protein and all that other stuff in them. There is so much newfangled technology those guys in London have that we've never tried, because we didn't think we needed to. We'd be better off, as well, if the prototype sausages were made close to the wise men and sufferers, so we can get better communication going."

A big smile appeared on Rhys' face. "By gosh, I think you've got it!" Rhys exclaimed. "You must remember the reason the prince consort chose your farm to visit was because you were experts in turning pigs into medicine. They, of course, were experts in the patients' condition and the intricacies of the disease they were suffering. Without you both working hand in glove from the start, it was never going to work. By focusing on keeping the prince consort's men happy with your data, you effectively created a barrier between yourselves that remains to this day."

Morgan hesitated and then ventured, "What about Evans Evans-Bevan? He won't be happy if we don't follow his advice."

"Leave him to me," Rhys said. "He'll see the sense of it when he hears the benefits."

ENDS

So what is the metaphor telling us, in a nutshell? The message is that Big Pharma's hit-and-miss approach to product development does not work in the long term for any industry, even pharmaceuticals. If we combine hit-and-miss with outsourcing of critical assets, we end up with companies not able to develop differentiated products—a condition now known as the patent cliff.

Big Pharma might just as well jump off that cliff now if it intends to continue building businesses with this crippling attitude. All that is left is to continue trying to squeeze more and more out of less and less. Eventually, nothing will be left.

The solution is not far away, as Morgan Morgan eventually realized. It is to adopt a totally different approach toward product development, starting with building a prototype in concert with medical professionals, patients, and other relevant stakeholders.

This may all seem far-fetched to some, particularly those having lived through the era of Triple F. As I declared at the start, I am a scientific dumbo claiming to think like an engineer; what would I know about it?

In anticipation of this, I have asked Jesús Zurdo to present his views. I encountered Zurdo after reading a journal article *Developability Assessment as an Early De-Risking Tool for Biopharmaceutical Development* that I had peer-reviewed blind. It was a massively impressive piece of work. He was thinking exactly what I was but approached it from the opposite end of the valley of death. I later discovered that Zurdo had cited my previous book in his article. We realized we were saying the same things from different perspectives.

Let's hear from Zurdo on this vitally important question for the industry.

AN EXPERT WITNESS STATEMENT: JESÚS ZURDO

Q. What do you believe is the major shortcoming in the process of drug development?

A. The industry still largely relies on a semirandom trial-and-error process for developing new therapeutic products. This is particularly the case in the development of biopharmaceuticals (protein-based drugs), where most current handicaps derive from the traditional linear hierarchical methodology (see Figure 14 below), in which different stages of drug development operate under almost complete isolation from one another, making it very difficult (and expensive) to solve problems once they are detected.

Q. What are the weaknesses in this approach?

A. There is a lack of robust and compelling criteria for the design and selection of lead candidates in the discovery phase (FIND IT). Furthermore, the existing processes to manufacture bioharmaceuticals require the use of living cells, which despite recent scientific advances are still difficult to control in an industrial process. This is why manufacturing processes often require being "locked" very early in development to avoid surprises later on in clinical and commercial manufacturing.

The process of developing novel biopharmaceutical drugs operates largely as a funnel, in which many different candidates are considered and tested until both candidate and manufacturing process are locked before clinical development in a point of no return. Here is where the "target product profile" (TPP) is defined. The TPP ultimately provides the label claim for the medicine. This label claim has to be set out during development activities. For the FDA, the labeling regulations are spelled out under 21 CFR 201.56 and 201.57 (part of US FDA law) and require the following:

- description of the drug
- clinical pharmacology
- indications (disease state) and usage
- contraindications
- warnings
- precautions
- adverse reactions
- drug abuse and dependence
- overdosage
- dosage and administration
- how it is supplied

- animal pharmacology and/or animal toxicology (if necessary)
- clinical studies and references (if necessary)

Hardly any of this information is available when the process is locked, so the TPP is usually built by testing the product obtained rather than by designing desirable properties into the product. In practice, this means that the TPP often drifts to fit what the locked process produces (basically 'whatever' the process is able to generate becomes the 'ideal product') and the drug that was intended at the start either fails or if successful in the clinic, often brings in itself a number of handicaps that can severely limit its utility in the world of innovative medicine. This is in spite of the large upfront investments, at a very high risk, before a product can reach that point of no return.

The industry, with few exceptions, has been oblivious to most of these issues for many years in part because of its rigid approach to development involving separate functions with little interaction. This introduces a high level of dysfunction in the development of therapeutics, where key design aspects are left out during discovery and where manufacturing processes are being delegated the role of fixer, which often cannot perform adequately.

Q. What do you believe could help?

A. In spite of such bleak situation, there are indeed a number of approaches that can help turn the industry's fortunes around. I will highlight a few strategies that could produce significant results in a not-too-distant future, some of them have been reviewed more extensively elsewhere[xxiii xxiv xxv]

---

xxiii. Zurdo, Jesús, et al. "Early Implementation of QbD in Biopharmaceutical Development: A Practical Example." BioMed Research International (2015). vol. 2015, Article ID 605427, doi:10.1155/2015/605427. http://goo.gl/OKbprX

xxiv. Zurdo, Jesús. "Developability Assessment as an Early De-Risking Tool for Biopharmaceutical Development." Pharmaceutical Bioprocessing 1.1 (2013): 29–50.

xxv. Zurdo, Jesús, et al. "Improving the Developability of Biopharmaceuticals." Inno Pharma Technol 37 (2011): 34–40.

- **Iterative or cyclical rather than linear development.** As indicated earlier in the book, design still has a limited implementation within the drug development life cycle, and drug prototypes are often rushed into clinical trials without sufficient guarantees on their performances. This is because the definition of a proper quality target product profile, which will determine the clinical performance of the product, is largely absent in discovery stages. Like in other industries, drug development should follow an iterative or cyclical paradigm (see Figure 14 below), allowing drug candidates to undergo multiple rounds of refinement and optimization before a prototype is assessed for clinical efficacy. Such an iterative model should introduce characteristics that are essential for the drug's performance, including aspects of the design relevant to the biological activity, safety, stability, half-life, mode of administration, target patient population, or even target product costs. It is too common to see products failing late in development because of issues that could be easily averted during the early design stages.
- **Design products for success, beginning with the end in mind.** This brings us back to the importance of the design in the success of a product. Some have argued Pareto's law being at play here too: that as much as 80 percent of a product's value could be locked in the design stages, which probably consumes less than 20 percent of total development costs. This is why it is important to assess and understand any important requirements for a product and its potential development risks early on. To help in this task, computer models are being developed to assess the suitability of a given product to fulfill development, safety, and therapeutic requirements and evaluate potential development risks. Equally important, novel surrogate analytical methods—such as high throughput and low cost analytics—can provide valuable information early on in development. The combination of the two has been shown to provide valuable help in designing and selecting the best possible drug candidate with the required properties to maximize potential for clinical and commercial success.

- **Changing manufacturing strategies: prototype versus commercial processes.** Would you define a commercial manufacturing process for a prototype before knowing whether or not it works? Well, this is exactly how biopharmaceutical development is done today, and at a very high risk. Up to 90 percent of products in clinical development fail to reach registration. This inflates tremendously the costs associated with the development of drugs and is profoundly wasteful. New development paradigms that use simpler, more standardized, and flexible manufacturing for prototype products could provide a useful context to develop better and more cost-effective drugs. It could even reduce the time required to initiate clinical trials, all without compromising quality or safety to patients[xxvi].
- **Use relevant preclinical models for safety and efficacy.** One of the main difficulties in drug development is the availability of good biological systems in which to assess the therapeutic and safety performance of a product before it is administered to patients. One of the potential safety problems affecting biopharmaceuticals is the onset of immunogenic responses in the clinic, which can be particularly important in patients subjected to chronic or repeated dosing or those with autoimmune disorders. Biologics can also occasionally cause severe, potentially fatal, immunoreactivity in patients, including cytokine release syndrome (also known as cytokine storm) and anaphylaxis. This is why adequate *in vitro* models, using isolated cells or tissue—often obtained from human donors—are increasingly used to assess safety risks ahead of clinical trials. For example, blood samples from human donors can be used effectively to map the relative propensity of therapeutic products to trigger undesirable immune reactions. They also can be used to understand the differential response to a given therapeutic across different patient populations and map the influence of specific genetic or pathological background

xxvi. Zurdo, Jesús. "Toward a Two-Tier Process-Development Paradigm: Prototype Versus Commercial Biomanufacturing." Pharmaceutical Bioprocessing 3.3 (2015): 179–183.

in the observed biological response. This methodology also can be used to assess the responsiveness of different patient segments to a given therapeutic, even offering useful data to define meaningful dose ranges for clinical trials. Such an approach has been introduced for the development of vaccines but could also become an important tool in precision medicine.

- **New approaches to preclinical and clinical validation.** We probably need to embrace reality and declare openly that we simply don't know enough about the biology of many diseases. In that case, it would be beneficial to change the way of approaching clinical validation. For example, it is still surprising to see how different biopharmaceuticals targeting the same molecule can elicit completely different, sometimes opposite, biological effects. Part of this can be addressed by developing the right preclinical biological models for efficacy. Novel genome editing technologies are now able to generate more refined biological models for disease (cell lines or animal models), simplifying testing and the interpretation of results. Still, more flexible approaches to clinical trials are needed. There has been an increase in the application of adaptive trials—which allow the introduction of modifications in the trial according to the responses from patients observed in the clinic—to better understand the profile of efficacy for a drug. Also, "Phase 0" trials—making use of subtherapeutic doses or local administration—are used to evaluate adequate safety in cases where a given drug could pose safety risks to patients. However, the industry should contemplate more often the use of alternative approaches, such as multiple branches in trials, to evaluate the performance of multiple alternative candidates when the mode of action is not well understood at a systemic level.

Obviously, these recipes are not panaceas but could help transform the development of drugs from the hit-or-miss approach to one that is more rational and sustainable in its way of operating, looking at product development in a more holistic way.

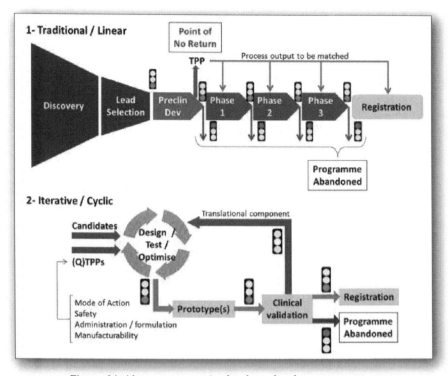

Figure 14. Alternate stages in the drug development process

Figure Footnote: Schematics illustrating traditional linear drug development paradigm versus an iterative one in which design requirements are incorporating early on as part of the discovery and selection process. (1) In the linear paradigm, a point-of-no-return (particularly for biopharmaceuticals) is achieved when a manufacturing process and target product profile (TPP) are chosen ahead of clinical testing. From this point on, any material produced has to match that original TPP. (2) In the iterative paradigm, partially successful candidates or prototypes can be recycled to improve their design; hence there is not a point-of-no-return as such, other than registration or termination in case of failure. This approach requires good integration among different aspects of drug development but can increase flexibility and productivity. (Q)TPP stands for Quality target product profile (see text).

ENDS

These are wise words for Zurdo, a brilliant scientist with a natural understanding of the translational issues. I would like to reinforce two points Zurdo has made.

First, it is not until well down the list in the TPP that anything other than a medical parameter is mentioned, and then it is the only one: how it is supplied. In practice, this means how many tablets or dosage units will be in a box or container and what the container will be. The multitude of other things about the product's makeup and supply requirements is contained within the common technical document, which is compiled by technical specialists focused on supporting strictly medical and clinical parameters. I am aware of no process to factor patient and other related stakeholder needs into the final approved product for sale. Because the label attained is the differentiator for the marketed product, all attention is focused there. Any one of those parameters that can outperform what is already on the market gives that vital unique selling point for the marketers.

The point being made is that the TPP is mainly a clinical document driving the actions of the developing company. Once the TPP is set, there is no turning back. The drug is on the conveyor belt to the end. What typically happens is that the TTP drifts away, often far away, from where it started as more is discovered about the drug and companies try to make the best of what they have. This is how attrition rates and me-too drugs originate—because companies have backed the wrong horse from the start. This is where Zurdo and I meet in the middle. The quality target product profile, or critical to quality attributes, will be determined based on those needs, providing defined parameters that the prototype must meet.

The second point is the iterative nature that is required to find the optimum compound with which to work. At the moment, the discovery teams walk away, as per our cartoon in chapter 2, once they "think" a compound will work. This crucial flaw has to be corrected. The brick wall between discovery and development is still there.

A brick wall is also, as we discussed earlier, between drug developers and health-care professionals. To explain this, we call back Dr. Gary Acton. We have heard his views on Avastin and the FDA, and he is no less frank in his opinion here.

AN EXPERT WITNESS STATEMENT: DR. GARY ACTON

Q. In your view, how could the industry engage more effectively with health-care professionals, especially during the early stages, in your field of cancer medicine?

A. The answer is that the Pharma industry will never engage more effectively, with health-care professionals or anyone else for that matter, unless there is a radical realignment of the framework, or rather straitjacket, which currently constrains the drug development process. The time has come to take on the deluded and deranged who freely roam the regulatory corridors of FDA and EMA trapped forever in their own weird world that bears only a passing resemblance to the one the rest of us live in.

Centralized command and control systems disintegrated decades ago in the Eastern Bloc. The Berlin Wall has collapsed and is long gone. Even China is toying with deconstruction and democracy. Isn't it time for a similar expression of populist freedom in the hegemony of Pharma-land? We need to tear down the Rockville Redoubt behind which the atavistic autocrats have sheltered for far too long and finally expose them to the light of a new era of patient-physician empowerment, which demands a reduced regulatory role that supports rather than suffocates the provision of urgently needed drugs.

I confess that I can really talk only from the perspective of oncology, although this is probably prototypical of many of the current challenges for drug development in general. One of the most fundamental issues we all face is achieving effective engagement of the disparate and diverse parties participating in the complex interrelated process of assessing a new therapeutic agent. The predominant problem is that clinicians, regulators, patients, pharmaceutical companies, governmental departments and third-party payers alike have no common basis for agreeing on whether a new cancer medicine actually provides a useful benefit—in other words, deciding whether it really works or not. This situation can only worsen as the technologies become more targeted and the personalization of therapies becomes more pronounced. The one-size-fits-all way we evaluate drugs and the inherent interaction among the various parties involved just isn't up to the challenge.

Developing a cancer drug is like preparing a complicated dish. You can have a recipe and make sure there are all the right ingredients, mixed in the correct way. But sometimes when you eventually bring it out from the oven and serve it up, people simply can't agree on whether it's actually done properly and how well it tastes. There is therefore the ever-present danger of getting your fingers badly burned.

Having cooked up a drug, though, the determination of its usefulness is a balance of efficacy and toxicity, and there is no simple and reliable way to measure either in oncology development. Efficacy end points short of survival are of limited value and subject to endless debate about their ultimate relevance to the patient. Improvement in survival, however, is a measure that is becoming increasingly difficult to convincingly attribute to a single, isolated drug intervention. We have become, in a sense, victims of our own success. We live in an era where the modern management of the patient with cancer is hugely complicated, involving sequential usage of many different treatment strategies, thus confounding the ability to dissect out the contribution of any individual component.

In metastatic breast cancer alone, for example, there are about seventeen individual drugs that have been approved for use in the first-, second-, or third-line context. They are employed, either singly or in various combination permutations, in the majority of patients with advanced disease. The clinical complexity of cancer care therefore makes it extremely challenging to identify and isolate the effects of one particular drug, in one particular individual, on the regulatory lodestone of survival.

Even if it were possible to definitively define the efficacy of a cancer drug with just one measure, the counterbalancing interpretation of toxicity is inevitably an imprecise exercise. There is undoubtedly a spectrum of individual views about what particular level of toxicity is worth incurring, for any given likelihood of benefit.

Science and subjectivism, however, are an unhappy partnership, especially when you have the regulator in the middle, in the role of the relate mediator. It may have worked in the early era of the postthalidomide aftermath of over half a century ago, but surely it is time to move on now that we all live in the new modern molecular millennium, where each patient is increasingly recognized as a distinct disease entity requiring discrete tailored therapeutic targeting.

Even the regulators in different countries can't agree themselves about striking the right balance. Given that, how can they ever be expected to find common ground with anyone else, including the Pharma industry and health-care professionals? In an era of supposedly increasing international harmonization, there are still a staggering number of cross-continental differences that occur when authorities in different geographical territories interpret the same data from the same drug, in the same indication, and come to diametrically opposite conclusions about the risk-benefit assessment. How can we allow such an inchoate process to continue when the only outcome is to support the dynastic dictatorship that regulators have come to see as their entitlement and birthright?

In oncology, at least, if we really want to improve the effectiveness of Pharma industry engagement with health-care professionals during the development of drugs, then we need to bite the bullet, deconstruct the role of the regulator, and effect a more direct collaboration between industry and health-care professionals, effectively bypassing much of the current restraint imposed on the industry.

No one wants an overtly dangerous drug remaining in circulation. If nothing else, you can't make money out of one like that, anyway. Drug development is also an evolving process. It's forever a work in progress, as additional information emerges about a drug once it is in the marketplace. New clinical trial results and anecdotal experiences gained through wider usage conspire to constantly change the perceptions of the risks and benefits of a recently arrived agent.

There has to be some way regulators and pharmaceutical companies can react to that, as and when necessary. Each party has to recognize the often-divergent needs of the other. When the interpretation of new information has the sort of subjectivity that nearly always characterizes cancer drugs, then there has to be a greater capacity for common sense and compromise than has been the case with the Avastin conflict.

Pictures of cancer drugs are painted in shades of gray. It makes no sense to adopt positions of black or white with them—or just black, in the case of FDA.

The geographical ping-pong of cancer drug determination graphically illustrates the difficulties everyone faces in making an appropriate assessment of the efficacy-safety equation. Regulatory authorities, such as the FDA, often find themselves out on a limb, as the case of Avastin in breast cancer demonstrates so well. They frequently seem to be predominantly concerned with protecting the vulnerable few to the detriment of the remaining majority.

One of the most fundamental of medical precepts is the Hippocratic proposition *primum non nocere*. This roughly translates as "First, do no harm." This is the philosophy that appears rooted at the very heart of regulatory review. By default, regulators aver on the side of caution, often giving undue prominence to side effects and toxicities. They want to avoid harm at all cost. Seemingly, they would rather take the risk of rejecting an effective drug than of approving a potentially toxic one.

But in the context of cancer medicine, where the benefits and risk are often so fundamentally interwoven, this is the wrong balance. It is leading to the sacrifices of useful drugs, such as Avastin in breast cancer, among many others. These are agents that have the potential to help some, through controlling their diseases, although at the cost of causing unacceptable toxicity for others.

And this is where, as many of the Avastin proponents have argued, the regulatory process potentially falls apart. It is impossible to make these kinds of risk-benefit judgments at the level of protecting public health, as regulators do, without fundamentally compromising the private individual physician-patient ability to make the same determination. With a growing future personalization of drug therapy, it is a dilemma that can only deepen.

This insoluble paradox lies at the heart of the intractable Avastin puzzle.

Cultural, clinical, and social issues inevitably come to each play a part in the assessment of new cancer drugs. All the inconsistency in interpretation of clinical trial data simply attests to the fact that, ultimately, the determination of whether a cancer therapeutic works or not is as much subjective art as objective science.

That, after all, is how treatment decisions are made at the individual patient-physician level. A doctor has an objective framework of his medical knowledge of the disease and the treatment choices available, but he also makes a subjective determination of what is best for an individual patient. This is based on, among other things, his impression of how well they might be able to withstand treatment, what their own views and desires are, and also the physician's perception of the outcome of different treatment approaches in his own hands.

While that works at the level of an individual patient, the problem with clinical trials is the collective nature of the results they generate. Here you are dealing with averaged-up data. This might overlook extremes of, at one end, patients who are doing very well and deriving exceptional benefit and at the other end, those who are faring particularly badly and being harmed. But these groups risk being missed because you are looking only at what happens in the middle.

Clinical trials tend to dampen down and mask out the range of individual patients responses to a drug. And this is where the regulatory process potentially falls apart. It is difficult to make these risk-benefit assessments, at the regulatory level of protecting public health, without compromising the private individual physician-patient ability to make the exact same determination.

To resolve this, it would make more sense for cancer drugs to be approved on the basis of some measure that showed on a balance of probability that they possessed useful activity. This would be much more appropriate than the current requirement of having to provide proof beyond all reasonable doubt.

We should be applying a test of civil, rather than criminal, proof to our new cancer drugs. This would act as a safety net but still allow us, on a case-by-case basis, to accommodate anomalies, such as whether trials were randomized or not, and to accept drugs that fall short on important end points, provided the overall picture of efficacy is a consistent one. After that, it would be down to the doctor and the patient to do the difficult balancing act of deciding whether the potential benefits outweighed the undoubted risks.

These are, after all, drugs that are ever used only by highly trained physicians who really know what they are doing. They aren't exactly the kind of thing you can get over the counter at the supermarket pharmacy. There's hardly a risk to the general public through making these agents less regulated and more widely available. And so for cancer drugs, there should be a devolution of responsibility away from regulators and down to the practicing oncologist in the clinic.

There is a strong argument for an even more extensive revision of the regulator's role. Agencies such as the FDA and EMA should perhaps retain the responsibility for ensuring that an appropriate program of clinical trials is undertaken, which is sufficient to permit an adequate examination of the safety and efficacy of a new drug. It's important that someone does that, and they are best placed to continue policing this. However, that's where their remit should stop.

Once they have ensured, to their own satisfaction, that there are adequate data to assess the utility of a new agent, this should be made publicly available, in a suitably digestible format, and then it would be up to individual clinicians to review the information on offer and make their own determinations of whether they see something useful there for the management of their own patients. To help the process, the regulators could even review the data themselves and provide a *recommendation*, although this would be no more than that. It certainly wouldn't be binding in the future, in the ex cathedra way these things have been in the past. A bit less Hitler and a bit more Hegel, if you like.

Regulators could, however, hang on to supervision of manufacturing and also postmarketing safety surveillance. Those are activities that shouldn't be left to Pharma by itself.

If we could ever effect such a revisionist revolution, then this would regulate the state to a more rightful role in the affairs of the individual, while still preserving a governmental framework within which drug development occurs. Removing the regulatory gatekeeper would open up the path to much more effective interaction between Pharma and health-care professionals and between health-care professionals and their patients. The fluid dynamics of such unfettered communication could only benefit all involved.

But achieving such a state of harmonious balance would require the FDA and other regulatory bodies to let go of a power they clutch so tightly that they probably couldn't release their grip even if they wanted to. And so, for the foreseeable future, we seem destined to remain mired in a sea of confusion, with drug assessments influenced as much by capricious chance as any sense of clinical credibility.

At some point, however, Pharma and health-care professionals will have to realize that their long-term interests (along with everyone else's) are best served by muscling out the middleman and reinstilling some rationality into an ever-increasingly irrational environment. It will be the only way to surf the wave of enormous riches offered by the molecular era, without being drowned, or dragged down, in the deluge.

But it will require courage, conviction, and creativity of thinking, as well as a bit of brute force probably.

To quote Einstein, "We cannot solve our problems with the same thinking we used when we created them."

And you can't get a bigger brain than that to point you in the right direction.

ENDS

There is massive food for thought here with an underlying theme:

> "You have the regulator in the middle, in the role of the... mediator. It may have worked in the early era of the postthalidomide aftermath of over half a century ago, but surely it is time to move on now that we all live in the new modern molecular millennium."

The world has indeed moved on. We all need to think about that and have the grace to admit it is time for all of us to contemplate change. Someone who is constantly doing that is our next expert witness, Bethan Bishop.

It was Steenstra who introduced me to Bishop when we were looking for an NHS member to help on our advanced manufacturing supply chain bid. Bishop has been a breath of fresh air ever since by speaking her mind and being completely authentic. Let's hear what she has to say about this crucial interface.

AN EXPERT WITNESS STATEMENT: BETHAN BISHOP

Q. You work at the sharp edge of the HCP/patient/drug developer interface. How could their engagement become more effective?

A. I note your question implies that pharmaceutical and biotechnology companies sit outside the health-care system. I don't believe they do. These industries are core to the delivery of health care and therefore are integral to the system. We should not work in isolation, be driven by assumptions, and remain in our historic silos. The challenge for health care globally is immense. Aging and diverse populations, inequity of care, all means we have the same challenge. We need to work together and stop being suspicious of each other's motives. Innovation through collaboration is fundamental to the success of health-care provision, a place where we take the time to understand the needs of end users: patients, clinicians, service commissioners, etc. Therefore, why would a pharmaceutical or biotechnology company not start with engaging the part of the system it seeks to benefit, understanding the voice of the customer up front?

Q. What would that mean in practical terms?

A. I would list them as follows:

- early engagement within experts in their field
- understanding the trends in health-care provision—the shift toward care closer to home, shaking up the status quo
- exploring what services need to bundled around new therapeutics in particular as we move to more precision medicines in better-defined populations
- moving away from a transactional relationship.

I challenge industry to get close to their customers, stakeholders, try to walk in their shoes, understand the complexities of the part of the system they work in.

Q. How do you go about building the necessary relationships?

A. I always offer companies in my network an opportunity to better understand how we work. This involves being exposed to how my colleagues think and insights into the barriers and benefits of working collaboratively. But I'll be honest: sometimes individuals and/or their organizations don't know how to react to or effectively benefit from that offer. Some are more used to transactional relationships with purchasers, simply wanting assurance that their product is suitable for patient use further down the development pipeline. They miss an opportunity.

ENDS

Having had personal experience of working with Bishop, I assure you she definitely walks the talk. I have seen her work firsthand as she facilitated direct discussions between drug manufacturers and leading-edge health-care professionals looking into the future of advanced therapies. As a result, both parties received astounding learning experiences.

Now I will complete our thinking on the development and commercialization of drugs.

Triple F must move to Double D

As Zurdo was developing his insights into product development in the industry, I was making similar noises. In 2011, *Chemistry Today* published a peer-reviewed, scientific article of mine titled "A New Model for Product Development." The article described a two-stage product development model based on building a prototype and then a full-scale commercial production.

The abstract for the article began:

"The familiar multistage model of drug discovery and development has been in place for decades. Attrition rates under that model have been and still are frighteningly high. The associated debilitating issues, such as weak patient engagement, limited involvement of key stakeholders at critical stages and slow routes to market, are clear for all to see."

The article is basically about redoing the mathematical equation that runs the industry, replacing:

F1 + F2 + F3 = $$$.

Where:

F1 = Drug Discovery (Find It)
F2 = Regulatory Review and Approval (File It)
F3 = Marketing (Flog It)

$$$ = Megabucks

With a new formula:

D1 + D2 = $
Where
D1 = Design
D2 = Deliver

$ = Bucks

Notice $$$ moves to $. It's not a pleasant message for investors, but some would say lower, more predicable returns could outweigh bigger, more elusive returns in the long run. Investors will have to make up their minds on that.

Big Pharma should, however, ask itself whether it has defied the laws of gravity for too long. Can any company survive in the long term with such limited ability to design and deliver products demanded by those using their products and services?

The prerequisites to this would be major, as the Big Parma companies would have to turn themselves on their heads. However, there is a precedent to follow from the automotive industry.

The automotive industry in the Western world may have felt fortunate when it was in a similar but less-extreme position around sixty years ago. In those days, the automotive industry was producing one-size-fits-all products that end users either liked or lumped. It was working to a formula that had delivered the goods for many years, placing customers toward the back of the line.

Then the Japanese production system revolutionized the industry. Toyota's leader, Taiichi Ohno, observed a fundamental change in the market for automotives during the 1950s.

He identified the following as the drivers for change:

- instalment payment plans
- used-car trade-ins
- sedan-type bodies
- changing models yearly
- improved roads

From that, Ohno concluded that customer markets were moving past the one-size-fits-all paradigm of the Model T Ford. Markets were becoming more segmented, and customers were increasingly seeking variety and customization. In effect, Ohno predicted the end of the "blockbuster" auto era.

The Japanese proved that the days of producing huge volumes to drive down unit costs, often at the expense of quality, were numbered. Customer was becoming king.

Accordingly, a new model for product development emerged. The message was to build a deep understanding of the value proposition that would capture the imagination of the end user and then build a production system to deliver on that value. The old R&D approach, often termed 'throwing it over the wall', whereby R&D paid little attention to the needs of manufacturing and supply in their designs, was deemed inadequate in markets seeking variety and customization.

From this emerged what became a well-developed way of converting the end user need into the product or service the customer received. To quote from *The Lean Toolbox*:[xxvii]

---

xxvii. Bicheno & Holwig, "The Lean Toolbox," Fourth Edition, P10, PICSIE Books, 2009.

"Taiichi Ohno believed in developing managers by the Socratic method—asking tough questions rather than providing answer. This is in line with the practice of Hoshin Kanri, or Policy Deployment, whereby top management sets the strategic direction (the what and the why) but evolves the detail level by level by a process of consultation (the how).

For a more detailed explanation, we call on Professor Nick Rich. I first met Rich in the early 1990s while I was at Bayer and he was at the Lean Enterprise Research Center at Cardiff University. He trained at Toyota in Japan and built a string of achievements in the world of production systems.

AN EXPERT WITNESS STATEMENT: PROFESSOR NICK RICH

Anyone who has experienced the process of traditional and "individual-based" management by objectives will probably have endured a bad experience. Basically, your boss determines what needs to be done and then hands you a task or a series of "to do" activities that must be completed before your next annual review.

Imagine if your boss gave you the wrong thing or you didn't really see the need for the tasks. More often than not, your boss is asking for a solution. "Implement this" is much the way management by objectives works. Imagine you are asked to introduce a computerized planning system costing millions of dollars when a simple reconfiguration with bar-code tracking would do the job at a fraction of the price and a fraction of the organizational turmoil.

Your options are limited under management by objectives and range from doing what you are told to do, to doing some of what you are told to do, to ignoring what you are told to do. Whichever way you look at it, and however you are motivated, the next review is in a year. Business can change a lot in a year. If you have not done what has been asked of you, then your boss has lost a year. Often, the boss would not even bother to review last year's tasks and instead move on to this year's issues.

Now imagine you set objectives at the business level and express these vital objectives as a challenge to every manager in the business— not as individuals, but as a whole. As a boss, it is your duty to think about the future. If you predict what the market will need in three to five years, you can establish a gap—a gap that must be closed if you are to remain competitive. This is the basic premise of policy deployment. You treat the business as a system. In this way, you can set objective challenges for managers as a group and the common key processes they control, such as safety, quality, delivery adherence, flexibility, reduced design time, better environmental management compliance, better regulatory compliance, and reduced product costs or reduced operational costs.

These processes are not owned by an individual department. Instead, they pass straight through the business and are the key measures that customers apply and how competitors assess your business. It is a fantastic way of encouraging management teams to innovate. The quality department never owns wholly "the quality". The purchasing team determines the quality of factory inputs, and operations and maintenance determine yields. So it makes sense to focus on processes. These processes link directly to closing the gap and have meaning and importance for managers. Managers understand the need to improve, and so does every employee, distributor, and supplier. Just by thinking about processes and looking to the future can bring about real and meaningful change. Most of us can predict what will happen in the market in the next three years by looking at regulations and other trends. Therefore, these gaps have meaning.

To really get the most from setting a challenge, you must establish a gap. You can do this by predicting the levels of competition and then communicating this as "the challenge." Let's say we must reduce new product lead times by 50 percent (from twelve weeks to six weeks in three years) and we therefore set the target as a reduction in lead time to eight weeks or less this year. Rather than imposing senior management's will on the teams — senior management set teams the challenge to be met. How will you reduce the lead time by four whole weeks? And senior management explain why it is needed and withdraw from the process to allow the teams—which know all about best practices and what can be achieved if everyone cooperates—to discuss the issue and find a common and agreed approach to reducing the time from order to delivery. The withdrawal of the executives is key—it forces the whole management team in one room to start talking. The first thing they will talk about is what it means. Where do we spend our time now? What are the failures in the current system that need to be fixed? After a while, the management team reaches some consensus and many departments will change their methods to speed up and create a quality-assured and robust process. The supplier-selection department could preselect suppliers, the production planners could release the facility for trials with only one week's notice rather than four. These modifications to business practice all contribute to reducing the overall time and eliminating the issues we face as a business. Who could argue that they don't want to make any changes? The changes are needed to stay competitive, and staying competitive pays our mortgages and finances our lifestyles.

Similarly if we are to reduce order turnaround times, the team may discuss holding finished goods stock, more work in process or other methods such as 'print on demand' specific language packaging, smaller production batches, quicker changeovers, and the like. As the whole team discusses each suggestion, it raises awareness and reaches agreements. Departmental managers can assign the right reports to the change program. The agreed projects (with timescales of nine-month stages) can then be communicated back to the senior management team, for discussion on any potential blockages or further opportunities for improvement.

Most businesses will select three major objectives, so this will stimulate more discussion to find the key projects that will deliver the necessary result. Let's say there is a second challenge to reduce the product cost by 5 percent and increase product yields by 10 percent for the next year. These three business challenges—to reduce lead time, improve yields, and reduce costs—are understandable and meaningful and call for the engagement of all business managers to design effective systems to satisfy these objectives. Once the senior executives have authorized the key projects, the teams can begin to work on them. This process usually is synchronized with the financial year so that any investments and financial requirements can be assigned as part of the capital provisioning process.

The teams start with the details of the projects and work on a daily basis. They report their progress weekly to the management team, which tracks the changes in the key processes and ensures they are on target to get to eight weeks to reduce new product time. Every month, a management review is given for all managers and executives, and the target of eight weeks is compared with what has been achieved or estimated as the time reduction. At the end of the project in nine months (to allow three months for a review of the business and the setting of next year's challenges), the teams finalize the projects and can celebrate. Celebration is important because any improvement—even if it does not meet the target—is better than at the beginning of the process. Any underperformance—say getting only to nine weeks from twelve—would mean the challenge gets a bit more of a stretch for the next round of the three-year cycle. So as the managers look forward to the next three years, they may estimate that the market would want a five-week standard of performance, and the new annual target may be to go from nine weeks to six weeks—the new challenge. The cycle keeps management innovating and talking. After all, most managers know the best practice in the industry and where to find it. This process allows them to promote these ways of working with the other managers to make the project a reality. So in the new system, the executives set the direction of change for the business—the challenge. The managers are vitally important and select the projects to help improve the business. Everyone gets involved with meaningful projects that require teamwork, research, skills, and a whole lot of fun.

It is easy to tell an executive what you are doing and why under policy deployment and how it fits with the strategic direction of the business. Let's take the story of the NASA cleaner. When asked what role the person had, the cleaner replied that "I am helping to put a man on the moon by keeping the workplace clear so the teams can concentrate on their processes."

Imagine yourself as an executive as you walk your business and see the walls of the departments covered with project team updates that show how key business processes are changing ahead of customer expectations.

ENDS

These words from Rich may come as a surprise to some, but this approach is at the heart of production systems. It is not about using tools and techniques to cut costs and create shortcuts. It is about taking a systems approach to the production and supply of goods and services to customer markets and being driven by the company's executive management. How many Big Pharma executives can claim a simialr approach operates in their business?

The world has changed for Big Pharma in the same way it has changed for automotives. It is time to take the same approach.

The following explains how the Double D approach would work, starting with Figure 15.

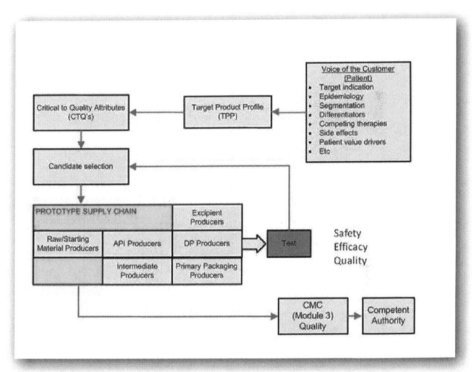

Figure 15. Overview of an iterative development process

The starting point for Design (D1) would be a deep understanding of the disease state itself, from the perspective of health-care practitioners and the patients they serve. The right-hand box titled "Voice of the Customer" depicts some of the many factors to take into account when developing a drug for a specific disease state (indication). At this point, there should be no focus on molecules, deep science, or clinical end points—nor any talk of the TPP because we now know this will decay over time. The focus should be entirely on the end-user value proposition and the quality required of the product when in the hands of end users. This creates a basis for the prototype.

Figure 16 shows the prototype supply chain defined up to the point where it is in the primary container for the dosage form, dictated by administration of the drug for that disease. This might be an injection, bottled tablets, capsule in aluminum foil, ointment in tubes, or other such delivery system.

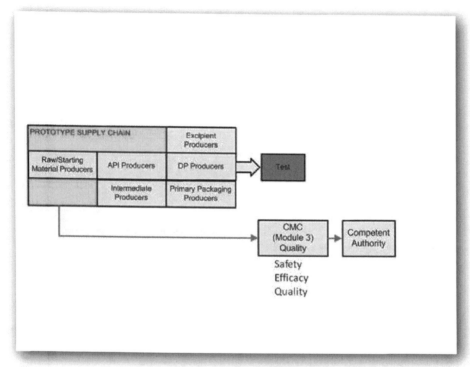

Figure 16. The prototype supply chain

Typically in the industry, the final dosage form is not known until well into clinical trials and can rule out a drug in development because its biological, chemical, and physical characteristics do not allow it to be converted into a particular dosage form.

The principles of the prototyping approach would be as follows:

- Design prototype based on full stakeholder involvement, including marketing, manufacturing, procurement, key suppliers

- Allocate overall management responsibility for the programme to market
- Discovery research stays with prototype testing - iterative
- Focus on manufacturability of compounds using predictive methods
- Build a deep understanding of material and process capability
- Institutionalise risk management into development programmes
- Build an outline of the end-to-end supply chain, using world-class principles

The important point to note is that the material produced by each prototype supply chain is subject to a level of clinical validation. We have learned that changes to a manufacturing process can dramatically alter the biological performance of the product and that the required testing does not always detect it. I am by no means an expert on this, but people such as Zurdo have the skills to work out that one, and it is certainly going to force closer communication between health-care professionals and drug developers.

Suppliers and contractors need to be involved in the design because they are the experts in what they do. They do get involved eventually, of course, but that is normally to remediate situations that could have been avoided if they had been consulted in the first place. Often, situations cannot be satisfactorily rectified and issues such as shortages of key materials occur.

Some may be surprised that marketing is included at this very early stage, when traditionally the marketing folk stay well clear until much later in the game. Forward looking thinking, however, demands their inclusion. Here we again turn to expert witness Dr Graham Cox for assistance.

Q. So is marketing getting it right early in Pharma?

A. Business has moved on. It is now at a new stage of Marketing, we call Marketing 3.0. This latest view is more than an evolution. It is more a revolution, which turns conventional thinking on its head. We only need to see the success of Marketing 3.0 with Google, Amazon, Apple, Facebook and a whole host of up and coming businesses that have shrugged off the shackles of conventional Marketing 2.0 thinking. As soon as you stand back and ask fundamental questions about what conventional Marketing 2.0 is based on, and the results it produces, it is pretty clear that we've all been ignoring the real data. Pharma being highly conservative is entrenched in Marketing 2.0 thinking.

Q. So what is Marketing 3.0?

A. Its not that market research is inherently a bad thing. All the top Marketing 3.0 companies use it to assist decision making, but the difference is how it is done and when it is done. As humans, we (and especially 'key opinion leaders') have a poor ability to predict how we will feel in the future and what decisions we will actually make, yet we as an industry pay tens of millions of Dollars/Euros to hear these views and direct key decisions. The questions and methods are wrong. It's not sensible objective business decision making, but rather an emotional crutch to allow Pharma to stagger on with the product to the next stage of development.

Q. What are the hallmarks of a Marketing 3.0 company?

A. First is 'Product design'. This is not new to most industries but Pharma seem to have ignored this fundamental process. To help companies make better decisions about developing products, they usually generate prototype options that have been pressure tested to give them some 'realness'. When faced with these, stakeholders make much better decisions. In Pharma, the old 'single TPP' model still lives on, to the amazement of other industries. The timelines from early development to launch allow for so many errors in trying to predict if a single TPP will be successful, adoption of the processes other industries use is well overdue. Marketing 3.0 starts with product design. However, where the Marketing 3.0 companies really succeed is in not jumping in to market research until the product design options 'look and feel' real. In other words, it has been really thought about, pressure tested from the technical and commercial angles and can be communicated simply. If one looks at the way that molecules are taken into Phase II, you'll realise there is little rigour and no real 'product design' thinking.

The second hallmark of a Marketing 3.0 company is confidence. It is interesting that the progressive companies seem to have an inner confidence that negate the need for old traditional hierarchies and conventional methods. Pharma seem to be on the extreme end of lacking confidence and a symptom of this is to reach out to market research at every stage of development for signs to keep them from being wrong. The driver for this is understandable, when we all know that patents (a good surrogate for product innovation) and revenues are plummeting whilst payers and government regulatory hurdles seem to be ever rising. But as the industry has proven, this is a false sense of security.

Q. So what should Pharma do differently?

A. If Pharma wants to significantly increase the number of successful products there are a few things that will have real impact. Firstly, an introduction of a formal product design process well before Phase II and secondly, regaining confidence in their amazing abilities to design and develop great products. These will help move Pharma into the new world of Marketing 3.0. With attrition rates as they are and the lack of real differentiation in products being launched, it's well worth taking a fresh look at where it all seems to go wrong... Phase I-II.

ENDS

Great insights, Dr Cox.

The fundamental of all this is that we start with a mind-set of success, not failure, with a view to converting the funnel that is the "valley of death" into the "tunnel of life," where products get to market in the manner in which they are intended. This means making sure the prototype is converted into a commercially available product. That means talking with the people who will need to bring it to market. It is they who should have the right of acceptance, or not, as the case may be, subject to meaningful dialogue and communication. If the prototype doesn't have a future on the evidence provided, then it won't proceed. The ultimate say has to be with them. Woe betide any architect who ignores the advice of those responsible for constructing the building. Similarly, it should be for Pharma R&D.

This is a complete reversal of the industry power base, shocking for many but the only way forward in our estimation. It is the way all other successful companies and sectors do it.

Figure 17 below shows the complete supply chain for the commercial product. Note that there is still clinical validation of the product produced, not a reliance on meeting predetermined specifications.

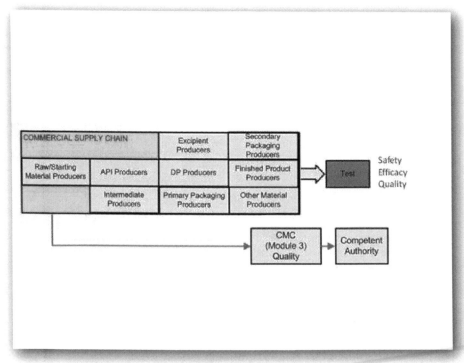

Figure 17. Supply chain development for commercial product

The key points are:

There is no distinction between the test product made for clinical trials and the product intended for use by end users on approval. Development and manufacture sit within the same team of people with operational and supply-chain competencies in bringing prototype products to market.

As it stands, the commercial manufacturing team receives a fait accompli from a team of developers focused entirely on gaining sufficient clinical evidence to warrant an approval. Commercial manufacturing is then asked to turn a hodge-podge of suppliers, specifications, quality systems, and all manner of other complexities into a working commercial supply chain.

If we were able to place the commercial production teams at the helm, the opportunity would be there to start with a simple, streamlined supply chain and keep it that way through the period of scaling up, out, or down.

The other suggestions here come from the world of production systems. The first was that quality (absence of defects) has to be designed into products and cannot be "inspected in." This is why it is so crucial that we have this simple two-stage model rather than three stages.

Holding the quality function responsible for failures only makes things worse because production could hide behind their colleagues. Responsibility should fall on the shoulders of those performing the work.

Quality functions can find far more satisfying work engineering out issues that lead to failure and working on meaningful improvement activities.

The final point is on the adoption of technology into the manufacturing supply chain. This has been a big issue for stakeholders and regulators for many years.

We don't have the scope here to go into the regulatory modernization initiatives in any depth, but as an indicator, Dr. Janet Woodcock at the FDA has been calling for modernization since before the turn of the millennium. Having looked at other exemplary sectors, observing how they operate, her plea to Pharma companies was to develop and manufacture their products as those other sectors do. She has called for "a maximally efficient, agile, flexible Pharmaceutical manufacturing sector <u>without</u> extensive regulatory oversight."

Today, over ten years later, regulatory oversight has never been greater, and it is still increasing by an alarming degree, as issues and misdemeaners proliferate and the industry culture fails to respond.

On that very topic, we move on to the cultural dimension of all of this.

CHAPTER 10

CULTURES MUST CHANGE, BIG TIME

Any rehabilitation program requires a complete change of attitude and a new set of behaviors. Readers may be aware of how difficult this can be on a personal level. It is the same for organizations and even industries. We begin with a metaphor to emphasize the point.

A Helpful Metaphor

Little Johnny and Jimmy are 10-year-olds attending the same school. Johnny has wealthy parents and has wanted for nothing all his life. Endless sweets and fast foods have been in limitless supply from birth. A visit to the supermarket is a joy to behold, with bags burgeoning with treats for Johnny. Jimmy, on the other hand, is from a family that has always found it difficult to make ends meet. Aside from some charitable donations at Christmastime, luxuries are few and far between. The majority of the family's food is grown in the garden and is supplemented only by basic necessities purchased at a local shop because they don't have a car. Jimmy is envious of Johnny.

One day, Johnny's father is deemed redundant at his highly paid job and the stock market in which he has invested most of his savings crashes. Suddenly, food on the table is a major issue, and trips to the supermarket are out of the question. Provisioning from the garden begins to seem like an attractive proposition for Johnny and his family.

ENDS

What chance do you think Johnny's family has of making that kind of lifestyle change anytime soon? They probably wouldn't know what a seed looked like if it got up and bit them. Nor what type of soil is best for the various vegetables nor how to prepare the soil, and a thousand and one other things they would need to know to grow vegetables successfully. By this time, Johnny is envious of Jimmy, who has grown up having to do his fair share in the garden.

Returning from the metaphor to the real world of pharmaceuticals, with patients replacing vegetables, Big Pharma has now opened the back door and taken a step into that unfamiliar "garden" territory. It is actually talking with patients. Will talking with patients help?

Talking with patients is a bit like asking the vegetables what makes them so big and strong. They wouldn't have the faintest idea. You would need to be a gardener to know that, and Big Pharma has never been a fan of gardening, in the metaphorical sense. Big Pharma has grown up taking trips to the supermarket to get its food.

Conversations with patients are necessary, of course, in the same way it is important to keep going into the garden to see how the beans are doing. That can involve some deep understanding of the needs that vegetables have, but it is a delusion to believe those interactions will change anything unless the family changes its ways. Yet there is no sign that is happening. The culture is reinforcing any attempts for change to accept the challenges on the horizon.

Winnie the Pooh Steps in to Help

When faced with a complex and confusing situations, it's often best to return to first principles—to go back to the drawing board, as it were. Who better to help with this than the master, Winnie the Pooh?

In his excellent book *The Tao of Pooh*, Benjamin Hoff explains the Taoist view of life using Winnie and his friends to get over the basic principles. Here, we consider "pu," or uncarved block. Pu is a Chinese word meaning "unworked wood; inherent quality; simple" that was an early Daoist metaphor for the natural state of humanity. In the context our book, it is about returning to natural state by washing away the dirt and filth that has been clogging up the machinery for far too long.

Hoff compares Pooh and his simplistic view of life with the uncarved block. This is what a conversation between Pooh and Christopher Robin might go like:

Pooh: Why does this medicine make me feel sick to my stomach?

Christopher: Because then you know it's doing you good.

Pooh: But honey does me good and makes me feel woooonderful!

Christopher: Don't be stupid, Pooh. If it made you feel wonderful, then it wouldn't be medicine.

ENDS

Christopher holds an assumption that was probably drummed into him from infancy. He doesn't question it because it has been there so long that he has forgotten about it. Pooh is under no such illusion. His mind is clear of any preformed notions about the way life "should" be. The truth may be somewhere in between the both of them. In some cases, medicine has to make you feel bad before you get better. But not to question that based on an unchallenged assumption is a big mistake, and that is why we adopt a Winnie the Pooh mind-set for this chapter.

The same is true for little Johnny and his wealthy family, as they "assume" life's luxuries are God-given and there for life. This is also true for companies, organizations, and even industries. They form a whole host of assumptions about the world that become ingrained and unchallenged over time.

Some background on culture change

Followers of organizational life will be familiar with Ed Schein, a brilliant industrial psychologist, and his work on culture and leadership. Those who are not may want to look up his book *Organizational Culture and Leadership*[xxviii]

In his book, Schein's work is applied at the company level but is just as meaningful when applied to an entire industry. In essence, Schein classifies culture at three levels. The first two levels (artifacts and

---

xxviii. Schein, Edgar H, *Organizational Culture and Leadership*, Jossey-Bass, 2004

espoused beliefs) are visible but do not say much about how things operate and behaviors are formed. The third level, basic assumptions, is the unspoken script that drives attitudes and behavior. The mightily important message that Schein conveys in his work is that organizations and industries can change in a sustainable way only if the incumbent basic assumptions are surfaced, challenged, and replaced by new ones.

To make the point, imagine you work in a retail outlet that declares, "The customer is our top priority." There are posters, slogans, and charts around the store to confirm that, and the CEO reaffirms it with an annual address. However, if you go to your manager to try to help a customer resolve a complaint, the manager tells you that company policy is "no receipt, no refund," or something similarly unhelpful. Then the message about customer focus is empty. The real company attitude to the customer is hard-nosed. That is what is ingrained in the culture and what dictates the customer experience.

Reviewing basic assumptions

There were many unhelpful basic assumptions in the auto industry when the Japanese revolution started. Some of the typical assumptions were:

- Customers can have any color so long as it's black.
- The more you make, the cheaper they are.
- Quality control can test out the rejects.
- If quality goes up, so do costs.
- Workers are merely factors of production.

This is where we are with Pharma today, dragged down by the baggage of basic assumptions not fit for the challenges of medicine in the twenty-first century. If I were to take a stab at these assumptions, using Pooh as my guide, it would go something like this:

- The starting point for new products is scientific discovery. This involves a relentless search by talented scientists, leaving no stone unturned in seeking out molecules that have the potential to cure unmet medical needs (blockbusters).

- These molecules come from a patented portfolio to keep possible competition at bay.
- Once patented, the clock is ticking, so press on as quickly as possible into the clinic. There is little time to spend checking the molecule for suitability to meet the rigors of market supply.
- The vast majority are going to fail, so keep investment to a minimum until late-stage clinical trials.
- Regulators hold the golden key of approval. Keep them happy, but tell them only what they need to know or ask for.
- Once a drug is approved, spending on mass marketing is essential.
- Mega-high prices are necessary because drug development is astronomically expensive.
- Side effects are unfortunate, but patients have to live with them.

Here we have it. The industry starts with a patented compound and looks for an indication in which it may show safety and efficacy. At this point, the patient doesn't come into the equation. The favorite indications are those with unmet medical needs, or "blockbusters" by another name. The focus is almost entirely on the size of the potential market and the net present value calculations that ensue. Those with net present values that exceed the threshold values, have some limited evidence, may be safe, and have some biological activity are processed through to development candidate status.

At this point, the patient doesn't come into the equation. This notion is captured nicely in the February 2014 edition of *Pharma Times*, where Kevin Grogan quotes Jeremy Levin, recently departed CEO of Teva, speaking at the FT Global Pharmaceuticals and Biotech Conference, saying, "The minute before you launch your drug, you know more about it than anyone else. But one minute after, patients know more about it than you."

Ask yourself, should that really be the case?

As a mental experiment, image a scene in which doctors, nurses, and patients are sitting around a table with Pharma drug developers having an open discussion about the drugs they sell, including side effects and possible alternative treatments to be developed.

No, I couldn't imagine it either.

Basic assumptions cascade down

The other thing about basic assumptions is that they spawn lower-level assumptions within the organization. Below is my own personal list of assumptions I encounter in the world of manufacturing and supply chain:

- Big is beautiful: invest millions of dollars in high-speed, long-changeover equipment to produce massive batches for block-buster markets.
- Campaign schedule: run the same product in campaigns because of the long machine changeover times.
- Keep machines running as long and fast as possible, even if the ones in front are broken down.
- Production make the product, but quality control is responsible for the quality.
- Don't worry; the qualified person is in control of it all.
- Suppliers should be seen and not heard.

In the same way, basic assumptions are formed in sales and marketing, finance, and all the other disciplines, feeding and growing off the top. This has led to many of the harsh realities we have discussed.

By way of further exploration of the prevailing basic assumptions, we now hear from Emil Ciuczak. I first happened upon Ciuczak when I read one of his many articles about the state of modernization in the industry. His views resonated nicely with mine, and I asked him to contribute to my previous book, which he kindly agreed to do. Ever since, we have communicated from opposite sides of the pond via e-mail and our various discussions in Friends of Modernization in the Drug Industry LinkedIn group.

Ciuczak is in the uncarved block camp we discussed earlier, where everything is boiled down to plain common sense. He challenges anything that is not founded in fact and has continued to do that throughout his long career.

He is funny but also a brilliant chemist with at least nine books under his belt on his specialty subject. He has been valiantly fighting the industry traditions for many a year. Let's hear what he has to say on the matter.

AN EXPERT WITNESS STATEMENT: EMIL CIURCZAK

Q. Tell us something of these "traditions" that you have been grappling with.

A. Unfortunately, the pharmaceutical industry, almost like a religion, cherished "tradition" over change or modern ideas. When formulation and production of tablets and capsules moved from the back rooms of the corner pharmacy to industrial plants, it brought baggage…I mean traditions.

Congress, in its infinite wisdom, assumed that a medical doctor would best lead the Pharma industry (because doctors had almost a full semester of drug information in medical school and were reading all the package inserts), and that a pharmacist (a two-year curriculum back then) should be in charge of production. Not an engineer, chemist, or materials engineer—a pharmacist.

Q. Can you explain why this is an issue?

A. Neither a medical doctor or a pharmacist has in-depth experience of the intricacies of manufacturing drugs in large quantities to demanding specifications. They just do not appreciate all that is involved, and while they obviously have a part to play, they are not suited to lead matters.

For example, my predecessor at one company, a pharmacist, had performed "vapor transmission" by filling a bottle with water and seeing how much evaporated. Needless to say, they were in need of a chemist to help them understand that water is **sold in plastic bottles**, so water, *per se*, is not going to evaporate *out* of a bottle, but *water vapor*, or, as you may call it, *humidity*, certainly can permeate *into* a plastic bottle and ruin tablets or capsules inside.

Q. That must have made you chuckle, Emil. What other "traditions" have you encountered?

A. Another tradition brought to industry was the plus/minus 10 percent target (of label strength). It was a carryover from the way "pills" were made (wet paste, rolled like tiny meatballs, and dried, not performed in more than fifty years) and capsules were filled (with a pile of powder into which one-half a capsule shell is tapped and filled, then mated with the other half). Apparently, no one at the FDA considered that maybe, just maybe, using balances and modern scientific methods, coupled with modern engineering, something better could be achieved.

Q. What do you think about regulatory modernization?

A. I am thrilled by the concepts of the recent process analytical technology and quality by design approaches. Mainly because I see good manufacturing practice much like I view International Organization for Standardization (ISO) certification: you can attest that you are doing the same things, over and over, but needn't supply any proof that you are doing the correct things. (That is, you are making it the same. Whether it is any good or not is not the question or purview of the ISO document.) Two of the good manufacturing practice clauses that have bothered me for decades are addressed by these new (to the Pharma industry, not to the rest of the world) concepts.

1. "Meaningful in-process test must be run." Until now, we did such (hah) meaningful tests as weight, crushability, friability, and disintegration. Not in real time and seldom on many samples. If a problem is seen, many thousands of tablets have been produced with the same flaws. Process analytical technology, when done properly, takes many, many, real-time, meaningful tests.

2. "A statistically significant number of final units must be tested." In the day and age where we produce as many as 5,000,000 tablets in a batch, ten to twenty doses are not statistically significant. When you get an FDA person aside (and add a few drinks), they will admit that making any company, big or small, perform twenty to twenty-five thousand high-performance liquid chromatography assays would break them. That's why, "wink-wink, nod-nod" the agencies accept current test levels.

Clearly, the quality by design concept would move so far beyond good manufacturing practice quality that it makes sense to switch. Often, the biggest impediment is the Quality Assurance department. These people have been chosen by their ability to slavishly follow company Standard Operating Procedures and Good Manufacturing Practice...their rigidity and, possibly, OCD, makes them perfect to resist changes.

That was a bonus when we had only good manufacturing practice to lead us. Now, as the Process Analytical Technology Guidance exhorts us to use our "best scientific judgment" and that each batch is "a validation batch," QA is having minor fits. Their entire existence is on following the "one way,"; and we are asking them to change? Perhaps education and time are both needed (as per Planck, "science advances one death at a time") for a brighter future. As a dear friend of mine once said, "You don't have to stay in business; it is a choice."

But, I have come to see important developments such as NIR, Raman, ThZ, MS/MS, GC/MS, LC/MS and many more wonderful additions to the archaic line-up in Pharma...I suppose I can watch for a little while longer.

ENDS

Readers may detect a certain hint of sarcasm in Ciuczak's tone. This is based upon many years of swimming against a tidal wave of resistance to new ideas, not only from the Pharma companies, but also from regulatory bodies and other key stakeholders.

We conclude then that a culture of aversion to change pervades the industry. As we have discussed, the only way to address that is for a new set of healthier assumptions to appear. There is no Ohno or other such visionary waiting in the wings of Big Pharma, as far as it is apparent today, so please accept my starter for ten below:

- Big Pharma companies are in the business of designing, making and delivering value-for-money medicinal products to end users; this is their core mission in life.

- The starting point for new products is patients and health-care practitioners in the primary- and secondary-care setting, with specific medical needs, often complex.
- The end-user value proposition must be fully understood and is the primary driver of the end-to-end supply (or value) chain, with all stages of manufacture and supply being aligned to deliver on that proposition.
- Failure to get a drug to market is not the unavoidable cost of doing business; it is bad. Everything should be done to prove a drug is viable before being tested in animals and humans.
- Side effects are bad, and every effort should be made to eradicate them in next-generation products.
- The key to regulatory approval is not with the regulator; it's with the companies developing drugs, taking the lead on patient well-being.
- Markets should be properly segmented, based on a deep understanding of patient needs and outcomes.

It's not for me go further than this, but hopefully it provokes some thought in the corridors of Big Pharma power brokers.

CHAPTER 11

LEADERSHIP IS CRUCIAL

I t is only fitting and proper to give center stage to the Morgan family on this topic. We join them as Rhys Rees returns to the farm some years later to catch up on developments since his latest advice.

Dafydd opened the door and broke out in a smile.

"Come in," Dafydd said. "Great to see you again."

"Same here, Dafydd. It's been quite a few years now," Rhys replied.

As Rhys entered the farmhouse kitchen, there was a surprise awaiting him. Neither Morgan nor Morfydd was sitting at the table. Instead, with a beaming smile on her face, was a pretty Welsh lass whom Dafydd introduced as his wife, Myfanwy. Also at the table were two children: a toddler in a high chair and little girl about five years old. Dafydd introduced them as Cerys and Aled.

"Pleased to meet you all," said Rhys. "This is a surprise, and a pleasant one at that."

"How are your father and mother doing? Are they OK?" Rhys asked.

"Never better," said Dafydd.

Dafydd went on "They both retired soon after we last spoke. Dad spends most his time playing golf at the Celtic Manor. He caught the bug after watching the Ryder Cup there in 2010 and since he's whittled his handicap down to single figures. When he's not playing golf, he's fly-fishing in West Wales. Mother is back and forth helping with the children but steers well clear of the business. Speaking of which, it has all gone fantastically well. Dad asked me if I would take over the reins to help shake things up here. He didn't have the stomach for it anymore. We are now really back on track after taking your advice."

"Sounds good," Rhys said. "How did it all go, then?"

"Well, we got thinking about these prototype sausages and decided to fly over to the far-off land and talk with as many of the wise men, and some of the sufferers, as we could. We spent weeks and weeks with them, following them around and basically putting ourselves in their shoes. We had a real shock. Our sausages appeared succulent at first, but soon there were complaints from sufferers. When they investigated and carried out tests, they found that protein deficiency was not as simple as they thought. Almost every sufferer needed an exact amount of protein in the sausage. If they didn't get it, the sausages either made them sick or didn't do anything for the condition."

"So what did you do, Dafydd?"

"We all got together with the wise men and developed really small sausage machines that could make individual sausages with different amounts of protein to suit each sufferer. We had to locate the machines where the sufferers were being treated, even in their homes sometimes. That allowed us to keep tweaking and testing until we found a sausage that was likely to work. We needed to use some of that newfangled technology from over the Severn Bridge, but it did the trick in telling us which sausage was most likely to work for which sufferer."

"Nice work, Dafydd," Rhys said. "I'm so glad. What else did you do?"

"We employed people in the village and surrounding areas to become experts in working the small sausage machines and all that highfalutin technology. Initially, we thought we could go on as we had in the past, using contractors, but we found it was too difficult to change anything without it costing a fortune. Also, they had so many other clients that we were way down the pecking order.

"We did have to give our repatriated fellow countrymen lots of training to get into the production-system way of working that you suggested, Rhys. It paid off in spades, though, because the new focus on the wise men and sufferers meant we didn't need all those sales and marketing folk and the guys who went out searching for new sources of pork.

"With the money we saved, we built extremely productive manufacturing and distribution supply chains for the sausages that got approved, so we didn't have to worry about the queen's favored period of protection. We could sell at a handsome profit by keeping our costs down.

"Not only that, with our newfound productivity, we started to pick up the sausages that those also-rans had been making once we dropped them. That gave us a more predicable income that we could bank on."

"Wow, boy done good then, Dafydd!" Rhys exclaimed.

With that, Dafydd's phone rang. He looked at the display and mouthed, "It's Dad."

"What's up, Dad?" said Dafydd. He listened to his father for a few seconds and then replied, "I can't do fly-fishing on the weekend. Too much going on here."

"Do you think you and Mom will be able to babysit on Friday night? We want to celebrate approval of our sixth sausage this year."

ENDS

From this, we conclude that a new breed of leader has to emerge with the mix of knowledge, skills, and attitude that Dafydd brought to the show, working to a new set of basic assumptions focused on the end users of his products. In effect, we cast Dafydd as a twenty-first-century version of George W. Merck, the founder of MSD:

> "We try never to forget that medicine is for the people. It is not for the profits. The profits follow, and if we have remembered that, they have never failed to appear. The better we have remembered it, the larger they have been!"

Coincidentally, Merck also took over his father's business and made a tremendous success of it. He proved it was possible to build a thriving business.

In recent years, we have seen Merck involved in one of the biggest lawsuits in the industry over its drug Vioxx. This is what expert witness Jack Shapiro had to say:

> "Never forget that we live in a post-Vioxx world, a world that saw physicians get mud on their faces and hurt their rapport with patients (not to mention their rapport with us, the industry)."

Another leader from those early days of Pharma was Robert Wood Johnson, chairman of Johnson & Johnson from 1932 to 1963 and a member of the company's founding family before J & J became a publicly traded company. In 1943, he crafted the credo:

> "We believe our first responsibility is to doctors, nurses, and patients, to mothers and fathers, and all others who use our products and services. In meeting their needs, everything we do must be of high quality. We must constantly strive to reduce our costs in order to maintain reasonable prices."

We contrast this with the horrendous issues with recalls in 2011 and 2012 at McNeil, a J & J Company, resulting in a 'consent decree' being raised against them, which effectively placed them in 'special measures' under the direction of the US FDA until they resolved the quality issues.

Many, if not all, of the Big Pharma companies have horror stories, and this is what the metaphor is telling us. Leaders in the early days of Pharma set out with deeply felt principles toward end users of their products. Somewhere along the line, the message became distorted. With the Morgan family, it was Evan Evans-Bevan's purported financial wizardry that started the rot, and so it has been for Pharma. Under pressure from investors to maintain unreasonably ambitious returns, these companies are wondering what to do next to keep up the pretense.

What can they do? The answer is easy.

CEO and executive boards must learn from the evidence and failures of the past, to point to the future. Investors must be convinced that their money is best spent catching up with the technology and organizational developments we learned about in our chapter on rehabilitation.

Having done that, they must take hold and start driving meaningful change in the industry by engaging with all the major stakeholders.

Sometimes I use the example of Toyota and the foot pedal incident to sound the bell of change among Pharma CEOs. As soon as they received reports of braking issues with their cars, Toyota's most senior executives were highly visible in the media assuring customers that they were on the case and sorting it out. As it turned out, an independent investigation proved that it was not the fault of Toyota; it was reported to be a problem with the floor mats placed in the cars at the dealerships. Even so, Toyota executives dealt with the problem from the instant they knew about it.

The first time I see a Pharma CEO on television explaining what is happening with even one of the hundreds, if not thousands, of recalls every year, that will be a sign of change.

Before we leave this topic to move on to patent laws and other related factors, we give the last word to Dr. Gary Acton:

"But [change] will require courage, conviction, and creativity of thinking, as well as a bit of brute force probably."

CHAPTER 12

REPLACING PATENTS WITH PATIENTS,
THEN FIXING THE SYSTEM

I n this concluding chapter, we assume that Big Pharma executives have accepted their roles as leaders of the charge for change
toward a new model for developing drugs, based on what we term
the Double D approach. That will require a massive cultural change
facilitated by the rehabilitation that has been prescribed for these companies. It is time to home in on the overall system within which the
Pharma industry operates.

VIEWS, OBSERVATIONS, AND PERSONAL
EXPERIENCES OF THE AUTHOR

As a trained production engineer with a specialty in systems improvement methodologies (industrial engineering), my career has involved
finding solutions to problems within complex, interdependent systems
of human beings working together to meet defined ends. I won't go
into the theories and models that have grown up in the world of systems
thinking over the years, but I will pass on a principle or two that I have
found to work in practice.

The first of these is the notion that cause and effect are more often
than not in completely different parts of the system. However, we tend
to look at what is in front of us and draw conclusions about the cause.

For example, if we take the UK NHS as a complex system, with more
than 1.6 million employees, public problems have arisen in recent years.

Hospital emergency rooms have become increasingly overloaded, with ambulances lining up to get to the hospital doors and long waiting times for those who have turned up under their own steam. Something had to be done. Waiting time targets were introduced immediately to force the emergency-room doctors and staff to meet with patients more quickly. That should sort it out.

Did it sort it out? Of course not; it made matters worse. Suddenly, emergency-room staff were watching the clock and devising clever plans to make sure patients didn't breach the magic four-hour limit. Any patient approaching the limit was sent into no-man's land, into a stretcher or chair in a corridor, or into some other status that kept the statistics in the green. In summary, it drove behaviors opposite to the needs of the patient.

If the people who came up with that solution had been systems thinkers, they would have taken a completely different approach. They would have traced through the linkages in the system to find out the source of this surge of patients. It wouldn't have taken long to discover that general practitioners (GPs - community physicians) over time had stopped providing extra hours support and that patients had a harder time making appointments to see a GP—especially in an emergency. The only surefire way to get emergency treatment was to go to an emergency room, where patients could not be turned away—even if all they had was a small splinter in a finger.

So we have the solution to the problem, then: GPs surgeries need to see more emergency patients. That would likely be part of it, but it may not be the complete solution. It's necessary to trace the process further to learn what is driving the changes at GP surgeries that led to the lines at the hospital. The root cause could be even further removed from the problem.

ENDS

The power of thinking systemically is that it leads to root causes of problems. It teaches us that the present root cause of issues in the industry are the patent laws and the consequent crack of the patent starting pistol. This has driven a wedge between the Pharma companies and the users of their products.

It seems ironic how two words can be so close together yet so far apart. One little 'i', strategically placed into the word patent, would be a simple transformation on paper, but the reality of it happening in real life, where the patient becomes the central focus, seems unthinkable. True, drug patents have been with us for a long time, but does that make the concept fit for a different world ahead? We will dig into the weaknesses of the current system.

When a patent is awarded for a molecule, it prevents anyone else—company or individual—from using that molecule in particular development programs. It's a bit like land banking in the housing construction trade. In this case, those holding the land will be pretty damn confident that they will be able to build houses on there when they choose.

Not so for molecules. We have learned that no one knows whether a molecule is suitable to make a drug. It may also be that other individuals or companies could do a better job with that molecule because of their superior expertise, knowledge, or resources in drug development, but are forbidden from doing so.

It doesn't help the companies patenting molecules either because they have only a finite number of molecules with which to work depending on how productive their patenting efforts have been. In fact, patenting molecules narrows the field for every player on it, hence the rush toward the clinic to get definitive evidence that the molecule works, and in almost every case it doesn't.

This is of fundamental significance for the Pharma industry. If there were a requirement to offer a much higher proof of potential for success *before* a patent is awarded, it *could* begin to catalyze and change the face of the industry. We learned from Zurdo that technologies exist to predict performance of a drug, but the incentivization to do that does not exist. Big Pharma companies are not adopting these technologies in any meaningful way.

A HELPFUL METAPHOR

Imagine some inventive individual, working in the automotive industry, asking to patent a molecule from which to make rubber that would help tires hold the road better. The inventor would be out on the street and told not to come back without a prototype tire on a wheel with evidence of improved road-holding properties. No one would see that as unfair because all the difficulties of proving the case for commercial success are still to be worked out. If the case is proved, then protection should be given as a reward for sticking with the theory, but not otherwise.

ENDS

A similar approach does not seem to be present for medical molecules. This becomes even more puzzling when we remember that nearly every one of them fails in a public fashion.

Following on with the systems-thinking approach and the critical interdependencies, we now look at the main players in the overall Pharma system to determine how they could support this radical change from patent to patient, starting with what more governments could do.

Governments need to go further than changing patent laws

If the first step is governmental change of the patent system, then regulators must do all in their power to reinforce the Double D approach to drug development. This would mean pressing some important buttons, such as:

- requiring companies to obtain licenses to develop drugs beyond the prototype phase. It cannot be acceptable for small companies, having never done it before, to have free rein to develop a drug for commercial consumption.
- requiring postmortems on all failed drugs to establish what went wrong and whether it was avoidable. If the company pursued a predictable no-hoper, then penalties could be involved.
- changing the role of the regulatory authorities from enforcer to facilitator. We heard from Gary Acton how they can inadvertently get in the way of direct communication of those who need to talk: drug developers and end users of their products.

- desisting from pumping money into a broken system. Globally, there is so much money floating around for science-led discovery research but little for genuine translational work.
- legislating the industry not as a faceless being, and placing the onus on the pharmaceutical companies to take the lead and become accountable. This could be catalyzed by giving regulators the authority to demand much greater evidence of a drug's performance (as described by Zurdo) at the application for a clinical trial stage.

The next important stakeholder is the group of investors in drug development, be they venture capital, private equity, or those managing investment funds.

Investors in drug development

At the beginning of the book, we said investors are the ones that have the power to drive meaningful change. The rationale is that they provide much of the fuel for the Pharma industry's drug development programs; the money to buy the necessary people, facilities, goods, and services required. The message is that most of their money is going into the valley of death. Invest in companies that are working on the ways that Zurdo, others, and I describe.

Setting up spin-offs, virtual, or biotech companies, where science and finance dominate the board of directors, is not going to get you to where you want to be. Those "promising ideas" are going to come under greater scrutiny as the industry crawls further into the twenty-first century. You need board members who are steeped in the world of the entire lifecycle of Pharma products.

Regulatory Authorities

If governments are going to ask regulators to adopt new ways of working, then changes are required. Along with a new approach to facilitate interaction between health-care professionals and Pharma companies (as we heard for Acton), they need to push for changes to good manufacturing practices that promote the adoption of modern manu-facturing techniques.

As we have learned, modern manufacturing has shifted the respon-sibility for "quality" from a specific overseeing function to those actually doing the work. It had a remarkable effect in transforming quality levels in those industries.

In Pharma, the regulations insist that a quality function should police the production workers, demanding organizational separation of the two areas. Quoting from the regulations in the United Kingdom, "The heads of production and quality control must be independent from each other." There is a disturbing presupposition to this notion—production cannot be trusted to make quality products.

In Figure 18 below, we see how regulations allocate responsibilities among the departments. Notice the nature of the "Quality = boss versus Production = subordinate" split of responsibilities.

PRODUCTION DEPARTMENT	QUALITY CONTROL DEPARTMENT
Produce according to documentation	Approve/accept materials
Approve and enforce dept. instructions	Evaluate batch records
	Ensure testing is done
Check and sign documents before passing to QC	Approve specifications/methods/ procedures
	Approve/monitor contract analysts
Check maintenance etc	Check maintenance etc
Ensure validations are done	Ensure validations are done
Ensure dept. personnel are trained	Ensure dept. personnel are trained

Figure 18 Split of responsibilities between Production and Quality Control

This is a 1950s approach to manufacturing that other industries have sorted out, inside or outside regulatory frameworks.

More worrying in Figure 19 is that both departments appear to be jointly responsible for most activities necessary to make fit-for-purpose products. If that is not a recipe for confusion and disaster, what is? It ends up with quality taking responsibility for everything (as the boss) while production waits to be told what to do next. The best that quality can ever do is sift out the rejects and attempt to "explain" to production why they must try harder.

SHARED
Authorizing/writing procedures
Monitor/control manufacturing environment
Plant hygiene
Process validation
Training
Approval/monitoring suppliers
Approval/monitoring contract manufacturers
Storage conditions
Retention of records
Monitoring GMP compliance
Sampling

Figure 19 Shared responsibilies between Production and Quality Control

This notion is hardwired into the industry and is further ingrained in Europe by the concept of a qualified person (QP). The idea behind this is that a single individual can vouch for the satisfactory quality of any batch of pharmaceutical production, even if it had traveled the globe and all that was available was the documentation that was filled in along the way.

I have written on this in an article titled "EU QP: Custodian of Quality or Piggy in the Middle," where I finish with the following statement:

" In conclusion, it should be said that none of the above could happen overnight, and any attempt to rush changes through without proper dialogue would be a potential disaster; but that dialogue has to take place, between regulators and industry, where all the baggage of the past is tossed aside and a new spirit of collaboration and common sense reigns in our industry."

Universities and colleges

We can no longer go on with the educational system for pharmacists, biologists, chemists, and the other life-science disciplines completely ignoring basic engineering concepts, operations, and supply-chain management. Universities and colleges are reinforcing the idea that the life-science industry is about elegant science and serendipitous discoveries.

As with Dafydd Morgan, a new skill set is required, and it involves learning the hard slog we all know is involved with true innovation.

Health-care professionals

Health-care professionals must begin to view themselves as the ones in control and start with a proactive rejection of sales representatives at the door, if they have not already done so. They must cease dependence on Pharma derived statistical evidence supporting one-sided marketing claims, and anything else that detracts from the patient/provider interface. They should then push for early involvement in development of the drugs they prescribe, if not themselves personally, then their professional bodies.

They must continue to get behind the likes of Ben Goldacre and others, as they seek far greater transparency in the clinical trials process and the industry in general. They must increasingly recognize the 'missing link' in the development of medicines today—their patients.

Patients

For patients, it is time to take a leaf out of Winnie-the-Pooh's book as related in chapter 10—become an uncarved block. Ask your doctor the dumb questions and expect sensible answers. If the answers don't work for you, keep on with the questions. As is often said, there is no such thing as a stupid question and the few minutes of embarrassment in asking the question could avoid decades of suffering by remaining silent.

A few years ago in my doctor's surgery, I asked him why I should take a statin as he was about to write a script. He flushed up a bit and referred to the statistics. Needless to say, the script did not make it to the printer. Now before you think what a boastful soul I am, there were many previous visits over the years where I just acquiesced to the 'doctor knows best' routine. It had clearly taken me time to pluck up the courage and ask questions. So this is not easy for most of us. Often physicians, GPs and other health-care professionals do not have a lot of time to deal with our problems. Not their fault, it's down to the system. For patients to get a proper hearing then, they must push back on the system. Those patients with the time, inclination and fortitude should hold their ground, especially when they feel their doctor is prescribing medicines based on one-size-fits-all information from Pharma companies. They also need to get behind their health-care professionals if and when they push back harder and harder on the Pharma industry.

The final call to action

In the latter stages of writing this book, as fate would have it, an event took place that symbolizes all that is awry in this industry. A high net-worth individual, Martin Shkreli, with a stunningly low net-worth moral compass, ramped up the price of a generic drug his company had acquired by 5,000 percent. Daraprim, one of the many drugs Big Pharma tossed onto the scrap heap years ago, increased in price from $13.50 a tablet to $750.

Readers will appreciate the impact this will have had on suffers of toxoplasmosis, the condition Daraprim is intended to treat.

Having read some or all of this book, you should now have worked out that the big pharmaceutical companies brought this on the world of medicine single-handedly, with their FIND IT, FILE IT, FLOG IT attitude toward life. It they had taken another path, and remained focused on patients not patents, it could have all been so very different.

As it is, the Big Pharma's are frantically trying to mega-merge, as observed by Professor Cox earlier, and invert their tax positions, in a knee jerk reaction to the crisis, leaving the door open to unscrupulous businessmen like Shkreli to do their worst.

There will be a lot of opposition from The Establishment of course. I was reminded of this starkly as I submitted my last round of corrections to the manuscript. A lady whom I had followed on Twitter messaged me back with a comment on the book preview:

'Good try but drug companies have too many lobbyists'.

We should therefore add a comment aimed at those lobbying to maintain the status quo in this industry. There are drugs not being developed today because of all the issues and inaction we have discussed at length in the forgoing. You and your families are not immune to one or more of the conditions that those non-existent treatments could have prevented or cured, no matter how much money you have managed to amass in the course of supporting what we have today. You have a choice therefore; either keep your fingers crossed and hope for the best, or lend a shoulder to the wheel of change that is crying out to turn harder and faster.

The final message is for CEOs of Big Pharma companies. Your predecessors discovered a wonderful way to build businesses, which could not be summed up better than by repeating the words of George W. Merck:

"We try never to forget that medicine is for the people. It is not for the profits. The profits follow, and if we have remembered that, they have never failed to appear. The better we have remembered it, the larger they have been!"

We rest our case.

APPENDIX: EXPERT WITNESSES

DR GARY ACTON

Gary Acton studied medicine at Oxford and London Universities, in the old days when study meant exactly that. He subsequently held a number of oncology appointments within London teaching hospitals.

For the past two decades he has been involved in cancer medicine within the biotechnology industry. He has worked on some of the most innovative drugs of the era and has been associated with most areas of the molecular revolution. He has extensive experience of cancer therapeutic development in Europe, the US and Japan.

He has served at board level in a number of biotechnology companies and is a highly sought after consultant in the field of experimental cancer medicine.

He lives in the countryside, in an attempt to avoid hand held devices, with Heathrow Airport as a second home.

MRS BETHAN BISHOP

Bethan Bishop is expert in creating partnerships to accelerate the development and adoption of innovation. Bethan is passionate about collaborative working. She believes innovation is delivered through partnerships which harness expertise across the public sector, academia and business.

Bethan currently leads Innovation & Industry Engagement at Heart of England NHS Foundation Trust, a large hospital and community based healthcare organisation in the West Midlands, UK.

In the early years of her career, Bethan worked in clinical development and consultancy roles in the pharmaceutical industry (Pfizer, PPD Development, Adelphi Group). 15 years ago she joined the NHS to lead the creation of the research management and innovation development infrastructure at the Trust. Bethan now focuses on developing strategic partnerships to improve services and patient outcomes through innovation.

Bethan makes a significant contribution across the region's innovation & digital infrastructure, including membership of the Smart City Alliance and Chair of the Innovative Health Working Group, Birmingham Science City.

DR EMIL CIURCZAK

Emil, currently at Doramaxx Consulting, has experience at Ciba-Geigy, Sandoz, Berlex, Merck, and Purdue Big Pharma. Emil consults widely, including with the FDA. He was a member of the PAT subcommittee (validation) for the FDA and is a former member of the PAT expert committee for the USP. Emil has advanced degrees in chemistry from Rutgers and Seton Hall universities.

DR GRAHAM COX

After gaining a PhD in neurophysiology at the Royal Free Hospital School of Medicine, London, Graham went on to gain 20 years experience in the pharmaceutical industry, working for a top 5 global company in medical, sales, local and global marketing, spending 6 years in the USA. Graham gained a degree in marketing at the Institute of Marketing during his time in Global Marketing.

After a year back in the UK, he left the Pharma business and he designed and delivered award-winning lectures to MBA students in London at the Greenwich School of Management for 2 years whilst setting up and running a few start-up businesses including his own illustration company where his work has been published in many books and top magazines.

Continuing to run these start up businesses, Graham then moved back into the world of Pharma as a consultant, where he now works for KASOCIO. Most of his consultancy work is in bringing 'product design' principles into Pharma to help increase better decision-making and launching products that people actually want and are willing to pay for.

Graham is a qualified Kitesurfing instructor and he spends much of is free time with his amazing wife Anabel out on the waves.

PROFESSOR ANDREW COX

Andrew, former professor and director of the Centre for Business Strategy and 1993. Procurement at Birmingham University Business School, is a graduate of Lancaster and Michigan Universities and holds a Ph.D. degree from Essex University. He was awarded the Swinbank Medal for outstanding services by the Chartered Institute for Purchasing and Supply, and is a Fellow of the RSA. He is a visiting professor at Birmingham, San Diego, and Nyenrode Business Universities, as well as president and chairman of the Advisory Board of the International Institute for Advanced Purchasing and Supply.

MRS CATHERINE GEYMAN

Mrs. Geyman is an experienced supply chain risk management consultant having worked most of her career either in-house for a large pharmaceutical company or as an outside resource to a number of firms. She is a founding Director of InterSys Risk, which is part of InterSys Ltd., a U.K.-based risk management and Information Technology consultancy that specializes in risk modeling, customized risk software and disaster recovery solutions.

Mrs. Geyman also designs and develops specialized risk software tools to support enterprise integration of risk management activities, including the award winning supply chain loss estimation and mapping tool, SCAIRTM. She is a Chartered Engineer and is a graduate in Electrical Engineering and Pharmaceutical Engineering.

DR DREW HOPE

Drew has been overseeing production of Advanced Therapies at Guy's Hospital in the London since 2012, which supplies clinical trial material across the United Kingdom. He is passionate about the promotion of ATMPs to treat the complex unmet needs of patients for whom traditional Big Pharmaceuticals are insufficient. His three years as Regulation Manager at the Human Tissue Authority provided the grounding needed to work in the complex ATMP regulatory network.

Previously, he was Head of Process Development at ReNeuron, and was successful taking a stem cell product to the clinic by improving production and analytical procedures and transferring to contract manufacturers and testers. From 1999 to 2004 he gained a PhD in Neuronscience from University College London, and was the Michael J Fox Foundation Fellow at the Mayo Clinic, Jacksonville, using cell modelling to examine molecular mechanisms in Alzheimer's and Parkinson's disease.

MR RICHARD MEYER

Richard Meyer is a marketing consultant with over 15 years of healthcare marketing experience. He has worked on the launch of some of the biggest prescription drugs and had developed some ground breaking Internet marketing solutions for innovative Pharma brands. He has an MBA from NY Institute of Marketing and lives in Cambridge, Massachusetts with his wife Denise.

PROFESSOR NICK RICH

Nick is a Professor of Operations Management at Swansea School of Management. Prior to joining the faculty in 2013, he was the Professor of Socio Technical Systems at Cardiff School of Management and an Honorary Associate Professor at Warwick Medical School. Before that time he was a member of staff at Cardiff Business School where he studied for his Bachelor's degree, Master's degree and doctorate. Nick has written a series of books and papers throughout the years and his primary research area is the design of production systems to enhance productivity. He was trained in Japan by the Toyota Motor Corporation.

MR PETER SAVIN

Peter has worked in the pharmaceutical industry for 40 years and is currently the Editor of GMP Review, a quarterly publication from Euromed Communications that informs, educates and supports the healthcare industry by interpreting regulations and related standards to keep organisations current.

He is an Associate in NSF Healthcare Sciences the Pharmaceutical Consultancy, Auditing and Training Experts and an independent pharmaceutical consultant working with a wide range of pharmaceutical companies, virtual, generic and innovator.

Prior to this Peter worked for 35 years in global, research based pharmaceutical companies, latterly as a VP Global Quality Assurance with responsibilities for risk management and corporate governance of quality and regulatory compliance.

MR JACK SHAIRO

Since 1988, Jack has been president of JM Shapiro Healthcare Marketing Research and Management Consulting in Maywood, New Jersey. His clients include the pharmaceutical industry, hospitals, insurance companies, and other industry stakeholders.

In prior roles, Jack was at Upjohn, Squibb, Lederle Laboratories, Pfizer International, and Ayerst Laboratories.

PROFESSOR DANIEL STEENSTRA

Prof Daniel Steenstra is the first Royal Academy of Engineering's Professor in Medical Innovation. He has a unique combination of skills and expertise in Medicine, industry and academia. He graduated in Medicine then worked in product design and innovation management in companies such as Jaguar, Unilever and Alstom. He is MD of

Innovations Factory Ltd, which develops and commercialises healthcare products including for near-patient testing.

Furthermore Daniel is the MD of InterAlign Organisation Ltd which owns and commercialises intellectual property rights of a complexity management system with application in a range of sectors. Over the last 18 years Daniel has led complex multi-stakeholder projects in academia and industry. At Cranfield he leads the Disruptive Healthcare Innovation initiative and research into the practice of disruptive innovation. Daniel leads Cranfield's biotechnology activities as partner in the Oxford BioMedica consortium to develop a specialist centre of excellence in gene-based therapies.

DR HANNO WOLFRAM
After more than 20 years in international Big Pharma, being responsible for P&Ls in headquarters, self employed since 1996. Consulting and change-projects executed in more than 25 countries on 4 continents. Multiple keynote speaker about marketing, sales and Key Account Management in Big Pharma. Author of the first textbook titled KAM in Big Pharma 3.0.

DR JESÚS ZURDO
Jesús was Head of Innovation bioPharmaceuticals and more recently Senior director of strategic innovation at Lonza Pharma&Biotech. He co-founded two drug discovery start-ups Zyentia & Zapaloid where he held different scientific and management roles. Prior to that Jesús pursued an academic career in Spain and subsequently in Oxford and Cambridge. He holds a PhD in Biochemistry and Molecular Biology by the University Autónoma in Madrid. Jesús also blogs occasionally at "Biotechmavericks" (biotechmaverics.wordpress.com).

Made in the USA
Charleston, SC
12 March 2016